D1216805

# SEEDLINGS
# AND SOIL

# SEEDLINGS AND SOIL
## Botany for Young Experimenters

C. T. PRIME and AARON E. KLEIN

DOUBLEDAY & COMPANY, INC.
GARDEN CITY, NEW YORK   1973

ISBN: 0-385-00577-6 Trade
0-385-05828-4 Prebound
Library of Congress Catalog Card Number 72–97258
Copyright © 1973 by Doubleday & Company, Inc.
Copyright © 1971 by C. T. Prime
All Rights Reserved
Printed in the United States of America
First Edition in the United States of America

# CONTENTS

# Preface

Plants have always been of interest to people because of their beauty and because of their practical value. Indeed, our lives, and the lives of all other animals, would be impossible without green plants. Plant cultivation has been an important part of the history of man. The development of agriculture has always been a necessary prerequisite to the development of civilizations.

Many people get great pleasure out of trying to grow plants, and in this way, they take a small part in creating the beauty that the plant world displays. Much of this book is concerned, therefore, with growing plants and finding out what is needed to make them grow well. There are also suggestions for activities that involve investigating the structure, functions, and behavior of plants.

Many of the activities can be carried out with the equipment and chemicals included in a chemistry set. Other supplies can be obtained at garden shops and grocery, drug, and hardware stores and through various mail-order firms. As a hobby, plant culture is less expensive than most, and much of what you will need can be collected free from nature's own storehouse.

Thousands of volumes have been written on all aspects of plants, so a book of this size can only be thought of as a sampler. It is the hope of the authors that the sampling will whet the appetite for continued investigation. As a help to that end, a bibliography is included.

C. T. Prime
A. E. Klein

# SEEDLINGS
# AND SOIL

# 1 | Growing Seeds in Soil

It is well known that most plants grow in soil. And while to most people, dirt is dirt, soils differ greatly and not all plants can grow in all soils. Closely examine some soil samples gathered from your own yard and other locations. It may be heavy or light in weight, stony or sandy, wet or dry, clayey or chalky, dark or light in color, easy to dig or hard to turn over.

However, most soils contain a high percentage of larger mineral particles, often sandlike, and successively smaller percentages of particles of smaller size, the smallest usually being of clay. Sandy soils have a comparatively greater amount of large particles, while clay soils have a larger percentage of particles of very small size. The relative amounts of these particles affect the air and water content of the soil.

In general, the larger the particles, the greater the air content, since there is a greater space between the particles; the smaller the particles, the smaller the spaces, and water is held by capillary action and it does not drain well. All this is fairly well known. Everybody knows that clay soils are usually wet and sticky while sandy soils are dry, although this is not always the case for sands can lie in beds of clay and be quite wet.

Material formed from the remains of dead plants and

animals (organic matter) is also incorporated in the soil. This is known as humus and gives the soil its dark color. For example, peaty soils are particularly rich in organic matter, for under the right conditions the peat breaks down to form humus. These soils are also often wet, for peat retains water well. Further, soil is populated by a host of living organisms ranging from quite large animals down to microscopic plants and animals. This multitude of microscopic life greatly affects the fertility of the soil. Relatively large animals, such as earthworms, make burrows and turn the soil over, but the smaller organisms bring about chemical changes that increase the amount of available plant food in the soil.

It might be interesting to test various soils to see how well different plants will grow in them. There are many ways to test soil, but for a start you might try the direct, simple approach of collecting soil samples and planting some seeds in your samples to see what will happen.

Turn the soil with a spade, breaking up large clumps as much as possible. Transport the soil in any suitably sized container. Plastic bags are very handy for this purpose. Note where the soil is collected, how far down you dig, and other factors, such as whether the area is shaded or open. If you are unable to collect soil samples, various types of soil can be bought in small quantities from garden shops.

Your soil samples should be sifted to remove large stones. This can be done with a garden sieve or a piece of window screening. It is interesting to examine the various organisms you are likely to find in the soil. A microscope or even a magnifying glass will reveal many interesting life forms.

Take a number of flower pots or boxes, all of the same size, and scrub them clean with clear water and a stiff brush. Do not use soap or detergent. Place a broken piece of flower pot over the holes at the base of the pot and fill it almost to the top with soil. Plant about ten seeds, taking care to space them evenly. If you are going to try a number of experiments with the same size of pot it is worth while making a little circular grid of wood that just fits into the top of the pot and in which you have drilled ten evenly spaced holes. Then you just spread the seeds over the surface so that one drops into each hole and sweep the remainder back into the package. Remove the grid, cover the seeds with soil to a depth that corresponds to the size of the seed, press the soil down firmly, and leave the pot in a warm place.

In any experiment, if the results are to have any validity, there must be controls, and variables must be eliminated. That is, all conditions except the one you are testing must be constant. For example, in testing different kinds of soil for ability to support plant growth, the soil samples will be different, but all other conditions, such as kind of seed, amount of water, temperature, light, and so on, must be the same for all the soil samples.

The choice of seed is up to you, but it is best to choose seeds that are small and germinate quickly. Radish, carrot, and mustard are good choices. Refer to the information on the seed packages for average germination times.

There is no set amount of water to use. The pots should be watered at least daily or when the soil looks dry. However, if you are conducting a controlled experiment, it is important that all conditions be kept similar except the one you are testing for; i.e., the variable. In this case, the variable is the soil, so the amount of water should be the same for all soil samples. All other factors, such as light and temperature, should also be the same for all samples. Keep a record of how much water you use as well as all other conditions.

As the seedlings appear make a note of the date and the number. Measure the height of plants every two or three days, count the number of leaves, take note of their color, and record the time of flowering. In this way you will get a complete record of the growth of the plants. If you want to grow the plants beyond the seedling stage, it may be necessary to reduce the number of seedlings in the pot if it becomes too crowded.

Table 1 shows a typical result obtained by growing a large number of radish plants and selecting a specific number of plants each week for measurement. In this experiment, the plants were measured by weighing. You can do this too if you have a sensitive balance. If not, use criteria such as the height of the plants.

TABLE 1—The fresh weight of radish plants
from germination to the age of fourteen weeks

| Number of weeks after germination | Fresh weight (gms) |
|---|---|
| — | 0.01 |
| 1 | 0.07 |
| 2 | 0.30 |
| 3 | 0.45 |
| 4 | 2.20 |
| 5 | 9.20 |
| 6 | 28.00 |
| 7 | 44.00 |
| 10 | 59.10 |
| 13 | 62.50 |
| 14 | 65.30 |

After testing soils, test for other conditions such as water and temperature. By growing pots of seeds in different conditions you will soon find out some of the essential requirements for plant growth. (You can even place pots sown with seeds in a refrigerator.) Also, you can repeat the experiment with three sets of pots, giving the first hardly any water, the second a little, and the third plenty. You can verify what seems to be common knowledge to all; that is, that plants require water, a suitable temperature, and some substances from the soil in order to grow well.

There are many more ways to experiment with the growth of plants in soil. At the beginning of the chapter, soil was said to contain different kinds of particles, such as clay. To show some of the efforts of these, you can grow seeds in pots containing clay, in pots containing sand, and in pots containing as many different mixtures of sand and clay as you choose to make. Modeling clay from an art shop will do. Sand can be bought at a lumberyard. Soil collected at a sea beach is full of salt and will not do unless it is *thoroughly* washed. Peat is sold wherever plants are sold, and you can try to grow seeds in a mixture of clay, sand, and peat, and in this way obtain a mixture that is more like a true soil. Try to find out if plants grow better in ordinary top soil or in your "artificial" soil.

Try growing a second crop of seed after the first in the same soil. To do this, break up the soil and the plant roots. Put the soil and root fragments in the pots and sow fresh sets of seeds exactly as before. What do you observe? You can also try growing another kind of seed in the same soil. What do you think you will observe? In this experiment you may see one of the reasons why farmers rotate their crops; that is, why they do not grow the same crop year after year in the same soil. Try the same set of experiments without the root fragments.

You can try further experiments with the spent soil left over from your growing experiments. Make it into a heap, turn it over thoroughly, and divide it into two parts. Spread one part out to dry. Store the dry soil in a dry place. Keep the other half moist for a month. Fill one pot with the dry soil and the other with moist soil. Plant the same kind of seeds in both. Treat them in exactly the same manner and compare the results in the soil that has been kept moist and the dry soil. What happens?

You probably know that various materials are added to soils to improve plant growth. Take some plant remains, such as grass mowings or dead leaves. Chop them up and make a very fine mixture. Add equal parts of the mixture to pots of clay, sand, and top soil and sow the pots with seed, together with another series from which the plant mixture is missing. The latter serve as a control. What do you observe? If you tip out the pots carefully and examine them for the remains of the grass mixture you added, you will find more of the remains are visible in the sand and clay than in the top soil. How does this observation relate to your observations of the plant growth?

By now you are aware that the number of experiments of this kind is infinite, and no doubt you will think of many more. Try repeating the experiments; for example, adding a small amount of soot or a small amount of chalk (real chalk, not blackboard chalk) or any one of the fertilizers sold in garden shops.

From much more complex experiments, but all the same very similar experiments to those you have done, scientists have found that plants require water and certain mineral elements from the soil to grow. You may wish to try to grow seeds in water and the mineral salts alone.

If you have access to the chemicals listed below, you can try the following experiment. They may be included in a chemistry set, or they can be bought at some hobby stores and garden shops separately or in complete mixtures. (Ask for hydroponics mixtures.) Chemicals can also be bought from various mail-order firms. A science teacher would probably have the catalogues of these firms.

5 gm potassium chloride (KCl)
5 gm potassium phosphate ($KH_2PO_4$)
5 gm magnesium sulfate ($MgSO_4 \cdot 7H_2O$)
20 gm calcium nitrate ($Ca(NO_3)_2 \cdot 4H_2O$)
2 gm ferric chloride ($FeCl_3$)

Combine the chemicals. For use, dissolve about a tablespoonful of the mixture in a gallon of water. Distilled water is best, but tap water will do. However, water in "hard water" areas may already contain some of the chemicals in the list.

Use the solution to water seeds sown in sand or some other nutrient-free material. To make sure the sand is free of any soluble plant food, you must wash it thoroughly with water first. Take a colander or something else with holes in the bottom, block it partly with a rag, and then half fill with sand. Water can then be allowed to drip through until it runs out quite clean.

Freshly bought sand is virtually free of plant nutrients, but it is advisable to wash it to make sure. A material such as vermiculite can also be used to grow the plants. Take extra care with these plants for they can easily succumb to disease when grown in this way.

As a result of experiments of the kind described in this chapter, soil mixtures known as composts have been standardized as being most suitable for the germination and growth of various seeds. These composts can be bought from garden shops, but you can make them up for yourself if you are prepared to take the trouble. As you read the directions for making composts, you will see why most plant hobbyists buy them from garden shops rather than bothering to make their own composts.

The basis for some of these composts is a mixture of two parts of loam, one part of sand, and one of peat. Loam is the most important constituent to make properly, and it should be done by cutting turf and stacking it in piles (it must be damp, why?) for about six months until it is completely rotted. Perhaps for your purpose any good soil that you can find might be used. The loam should be sifted and mixed with the sand. Peat can be purchased and this too should be sifted.

The composts sold at stores have been sterilized to kill the spores of pests and diseases in the soil, but this is difficult to do with any large quantity of soil at home. Basically, the process consists of heating the soil to about the boiling point of water or above. You can try small quantities in a pressure cooker if you have one, or even in an oven. If you do try, the loam must be dry to begin with—not wet. You need only sterilize the loam, and although you can sterilize the sand and loam together, you cannot sterilize the whole compost mixture, as chemical changes go on that make it much less suitable for plant growth. For instance, the amount of nitrogen available can be increased to a level too high for good seedling growth.

To complete the compost, it is necessary to add one and a half ounces of superphosphate and three-quarters of an ounce of chalk to every bushel of soil; two or three pailfuls may be taken as equal to a bushel. The compost will be found suitable for growing the seeds of many common garden vegetable plants. You can try growth experiments with this compost. Various composts have been devised for different growing situations. Ask about these in garden shops.

With these composts you can go on to try to raise the seedlings of as many kinds of plants as you choose. You may also wish to try the seeds of some wild plants, in which case you may meet some different patterns of germination behavior. Some seeds require very special conditions for germination, which are discussed in later chapters. You can also try to germinate some common seeds of plants bought as food in grocery stores—walnuts and other nuts, date stones, and orange pits, for example. You may well find that some of them, especially date and orange seeds, require a really hot place like the top of a radiator to get them started.

# 2 | More About Plant Nutrition

You will have gathered from the first chapter that plants not only require certain mineral nutrients to grow, but also that they require them in different amounts and proportions. Some, like many of our important crop plants, require large amounts of nutrients, while others are able to grow well with a much smaller supply of nutrients. This is one of the reasons why some wild plants are only to be found in rich soils, while others flourish in very poor soils.

Test the effect of adding small quantities (a teaspoonful or less) of potash (potassium sulfate or chloride) to tomato seedlings in pots, keeping other plants from the same batch as a control. Try a similar experiment, adding small quantities of ammonium sulfate to cabbage seedlings grown singly in pots, again keeping some seedlings from the same batch as controls. In the second experiment you may find that the cabbage plants become rather dark green in color and coarse in growth. These are the effects of overfertilizing with nitrogen, and you can often see similar symptoms in plants growing on manure heaps.

Deficiency symptoms caused by too little nitrogen are also common. Stunted growth, early flowering, and the presence of reddish tints in the older leaves are the chief signs to be looked for. They may be seen in plants growing in extreme conditions, such as on gravel or the tops of walls, or in vegetables growing in very poor soil.

The deficiency symptoms caused by lack of adequate minerals can each be recognized by an expert as easily as the diseases caused in man by a lack of adequate vitamins. Knowledge of the exact requirements of crop plants is very important for it is obviously the way to greater yields and more food for human consumption.

However, getting plants to grow well is not entirely a matter of having mineral nutrients in the soil. They may be present in the soil, but for some reason or another the plant may be unable to take them up. There are several reasons for this, and one of the most important is concerned with soil acidity. Chalky (limy) soils are alkaline, and bogs are acid. They are very different soils and they support very different plants, and the difference in acidity in part accounts for this.

Acidity is due to the concentrations of hydrogen ions (see a chemistry book for further explanation), and at a concentration of $10^{-7}$ the reaction is neutral. This concentration is written on what is usually called the pH scale, as pH=7.0. If the concentration increases, the pH figure decreases; thus pH 6.0 means a concentration of hydrogen ions ten times as great as that of pH 7.0. Chalky soils have a pH of the order of 8.0, while boggy soils may have a pH of 4.0. This is easily measured by the use of indicators, and you can buy kits for measuring the pH of soils. All soil pH tests involve observing a color change in an indicator. Follow the directions included with the kit.

It is possible to grow plants without soil in various nutrient solutions. The plants can be grown supported in materials such as sand or vermiculite watered with nutrient solutions as described in the previous chapter. It is also possible to grow plants in the solutions alone. This is an interesting and challenging activity. You can also do further experiments leaving out one or another mineral nutrient and seeing what happens.

The basic idea is to dissolve certain mixtures of mineral salts, such as described on page 6, in water and to grow plants in the solution alone rather than in soil. The mineral mixture described on page 6 is only one of many possibilities. Two more are given here.

1.0 gm potassium nitrate ($KNO_3$)
0.5 gm sodium chloride (NaCl)
0.5 gm calcium sulfate ($CaSO_4$)
0.5 gm magnesium sulfate ($MgSO_4$)
0.5 gm calcium phosphate ($Ca_3(PO_4)_2$)
a trace of 10 percent iron chloride ($FeCl_3$) solution
Dissolve in a liter of distilled water.

0.8 gm calcium nitrate ($Ca(NO_3)_2$)
0.2 gm potassium nitrate ($KNO_3$)
0.2 gm potassium acid phosphate ($KH_2PO_4$) (dibasic)
0.2 gm magnesium sulfate ($MgSO_4 \cdot 7H_2O$)
0.2 gm potassium chloride (KCl)
a trace of 1 percent iron chloride ($FeCl_3$) solution
Dissolve in a liter of distilled water.

If you do not have a laboratory balance, it is far more expedient to purchase ready-made mineral mixtures. It is sometimes necessary to add buffers to the solutions to get them to proper pH. Making the buffers is a complicated business and is one more argument in favor of using pre-prepared mixtures. If you have the time and inclination, you can prepare the buffers, following the instructions in Appendix II.

Get some large, wide-mouthed jars that hold about two quarts. Wash them thoroughly with a detergent and rinse them several times with water to make sure that they are absolutely clean. Make a dark paper or aluminum foil wrapper that will fit around each jar and keep out light. This is to prevent the growth of algae. The wrapper should slip off easily so that you can see how root growth is proceeding.

As you might expect, one of the problems is to devise a means of supporting the plants so that the roots are in the water and the rest of the plant is not. There are many ways to do this, and what follows is only one of a variety of methods.

Make a cover that will fit the top of the jar. If you are lucky enough to find a cork that will fit, use that. Or cut a piece of plywood (¼″ to ⅜″ thickness is best) that is slightly larger than the jar opening. Drill holes in the cork or wood of suitable size to support the plant stems. To effect a tight seal, dip the surface that is to be placed in contact with the mouth of the jar in molten paraffin. Press it onto the top of the jar and allow to set. Break through the holes. The top will have to be resealed whenever the top is taken off for any reason. (See below.) A paraffin seal may not be necessary with a tight fitting cork.

Grow some seedlings like barley or sunflower in sand or vermiculite, as described in the previous chapter, until they are an inch or two high. Take three sturdy ones and fit them into the holes of the cover (Figure 1), packing around them enough cotton to hold them firmly in position. It is very

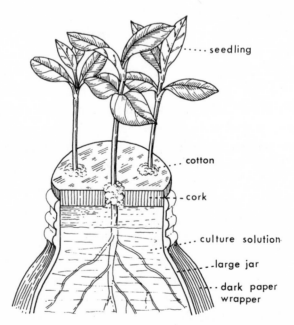

FIGURE 1. *Growth of seedlings in culture solution.*

important that the cotton not make contact with the solution, for it will draw it up and wet the surface of the seedling so that it may rot and die.

Fill the jars to about ½" from the top. Before finally placing the seedlings in the solution, check the acidity and shake the solution well so that it is aerated. The pH of the solution should be between 4.5 and 6.5. If it is not, an error was probably made in the preparation. As the seedlings grow, water will pass out through the plants, and the solution will tend to become alkaline. The solution should be changed at least once a week, or more often if the water level drops below the roots, or if the pH goes beyond the desired range. Test the pH daily. One way of doing this is to have an extra hole in the cover, sealed with paraffin or even chewing gum. To test, break the seal and dip a clean glass rod into the solution. Pull it out and touch it to some pH indicator paper. Don't forget to reseal the hole. When replacing the cover, heat the paraffin on the rim of the jar top, rather than the cover, to avoid damaging the seedlings.

With patience you can grow plants to full maturity with these techniques.

The effect of soil acidity can be direct or indirect. One well-known indirect effect of soil alkalinity caused by the calcium in chalky soils is that iron gets locked up in the soil and becomes unavailable to the plant. Since iron is necessary for the formation of chlorophyll, the leaves of plants in these growing conditions turn a yellow-green, a condition known as chlorosis. Careful search of plants growing on chalky soils in nature will usually reveal leaves showing this condition. To add more iron to the soil is useless, for it just gets changed into insoluble iron phosphates or hydroxides to add to those already there. Recently, chemicals have been found that get over the difficulty. They are known as chelates or sequestrenes, and in these the iron is united with an organic compound that alters its properties slightly. The metallic portion is retained so that phosphates and hydroxides are not produced, and the iron remains available to the plant.

The difference can be shown very clearly if a little iron sulfate is dissolved in water and a solution of lime added. A bulky brown insoluble precipitate is formed and this is what happens in limy soils. If some sequestrene iron compound (it may be purchased under this name) is treated in the same way, no precipitate is formed.

The effect of this compound on the growth of plants is most pronounced in the case of so-called lime-hating or calcifuge plants like heathers and rhododendrons, which so often show symptoms of chlorosis when attempts are made to grow them in limy soils. When sequestrene is added to the soil at a strength of 1 in 1,000 the chlorotic symptoms usually disappear in a short space of time. Tomatoes and egg plants respond favorably to sequestrenes and are good plants to use for an experiment. Grow batches of each in chalky soil and similar soil to which sequestrene has been added.

In general, it seems that other mineral nutrients, like manganese, may also be made unavailable at high pH levels. Not so molybdenum, which is made more available at high pH. Iron is made unavailable when it is turned to insoluble phosphate or hydroxide. You might expect that fertilizing with phosphate would, at high pH, tend to make iron unavailable, and such is indeed the case. This is but one example of the many complexities of plant nutrition.

Another indirect effect is seen at the other end of the pH scale. When soils become acid, substances may be brought into solution that may benefit the plant, but there are others that may be more or less toxic to plants. Chickweed and dandelion are quite tolerant to acidity, but the effect of acidity on a clay soil is to increase the solubility of aluminum to which these plants are sensitive. Consequently, they are rare in such soils, but in acid sandy soils with little aluminum they may be common. This can be shown by growing these plants in washed clean sand, as described on page 5, kept wet with a nutrient solution plus a dilute solution of aluminum sulfate (about .05 percent), keeping, as before, a set of plants as controls.

Other mineral elements in the soil are more directly toxic than aluminum. Lead and other heavy metals are particularly so, and very few plants can tolerate them in any quantity. There are some plants that can tolerate lead. Among these are the spring sandwort (*Minuartia verna*) and a form of alpine penny cress (*Thlaspi alpestre*) which are found in the neighborhood of lead mines. The toxicity of lead for most plants accounts for the ugliness of the land in some mining districts on which almost nothing seems able to grow. Much research is going into the problem of reclaiming such areas, and the chief hope seems to lie in finding varieties of grasses and similar plants that are tolerant of relatively large quantities of these heavy metals and then establishing them with the help of balanced fertilizers.

Lastly, an effect of soil on flower color is worthy of mention. The commonly grown hydrangea has flowers that are normally rose red, but when the plants are grown in acid soils they turn a deep blue. Apparently, these colors depend on the presence of aluminum in the flower buds before opening. The blue color can be obtained by adding soluble aluminum sulfate to the soil, and as we have seen, in the presence of acids the aluminum is released and is available to the plant. Conversely, the pink color can be retained by adding lime which tends to lock up the available aluminum in the soil. If you have any hydrangea plants you can experiment with them.

# 3 | Different Kinds of Seeds and Their Structures

Seeds contain a baby plant, or embryo, and stored food to maintain the plant until it develops leaves. This is enclosed in a protective coat called the testa. This is a simple enough statement, but within it there is room for an infinite variety of structure, size, and pattern.

A soaked pea or bean demonstrates a typical seed structure: an outside covering, the testa, that can be easily pulled off, inside of which are two parts that readily separate. These are the seed leaves (called cotyledons) which contain the food reserve, while between them a little search will reveal a tiny shoot called the plumule and a rather larger and longer rootlet called the radicle. The seed leaves are attached to these, for only through the cotyledonary stalks can the food reserve ever reach the tiny plumule or radicle (Figure 2).

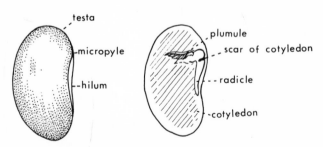

FIGURE 2.   *Structure of bean seed.*

The flowering plants are divided into two large groups, the dicotyledons and monocotyledons having two and one cotyledons respectively. For example, beans and peas are dicotyledons, while corn and all the grains are monocotyledons. Many seeds store the food reserve in a tissue separate from the embryo, in which case the cotyledons and often the whole embryo are very small, for the bulk of the seed is the food reserve, or endosperm, as it is called. The majority of the monocotyledon seeds are endospermous, but both kinds are widely represented in the dicotyledons.

To see something of the variation in seed structure, buy several packages of seeds and soak a few seeds of each for twenty-four hours or so. Buy packages of large seeds, for they are obviously easier to investigate. For very small seeds it may be necessary to use a magnifying glass or microscope. Collect, or, if necessary, buy many other seeds, not usually sold in packages, such as apple and lemon seeds, date and plum stones, and various nuts and soak them in the same way. Then, with the aid of a penknife and some dissecting needles, try to pull them apart and observe their structure. In general, it is better to try to pry the seeds apart rather than to cut them. They may naturally separate into their component parts.

In the flowering plants the seeds are always contained in a fruit of some kind; we usually think of a fruit as being fleshy or succulent, but it can be hard or woody. Many of what we call vegetables are fruits. An acorn is really a single-seeded fruit, and if you break the outer fruit wall off, you will find the seed inside. You may also be able to find the small radicle and plumule at one end of it (Figure 3). Most of the seed is made up of the two cotyledons. A hazel nut is much the same as an acorn, although in it the cotyledons stick together and are harder to pry apart.

There are, however, "seeds" that are really fruits. The seeds of the sunflower are fruits, and in all the grains (grasses) there are one-seeded fruits in which the fruit and seed wall have completely fused together. Corn is an excel-

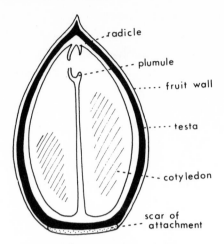

FIGURE 3.    *Structure of the acorn.*

lent example to study, but in many grasses, not only have seed and fruit wall joined together, but other parts of the flower remain attached to the fruit when it leaves the parent plant, so that it may be quite a complicated structure.

In berries the whole of the fruit wall is fleshy and the seeds are ultimately free in the flesh; the tomato is one of the best examples and, botanically speaking, fruits like squashes and oranges, are all berries. Stone fruits (drupes) are different, for here the inner fruit wall is woody and the seed is within this stone. Almonds and plums are excellent examples; crack the stones in each case to find the seed. Other fruits split into parts which each contain a seed. The fruits of the parsley family will all split into two halves, while the fruits of the hollyhock divide into many sections, each containing one seed (Figure 4).

Variation in seeds is also great, although the structures are harder to see in small seeds. Seed coats themselves are different, for some are hard and shiny while others are slimy and mucilaginous. Try soaking some seeds of linseed and watching, with the help of a microscope, the testas swell (see Chapter 14). Great swelling occurs in the cells of the testa

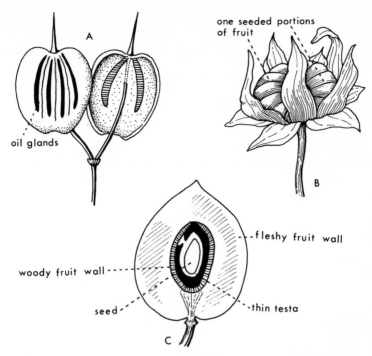

FIGURE 4. *Fruits of (a) member of parsley family splitting into two one-seeded parts (b) hollyhock splitting into many one-seeded parts (c) plum.*

and the mucilage protrudes in long columns with many thickening spirals derived from the cell walls among them. Soaked seeds of plants such as *Gilia, Cobaea,* and *Collomia* are also quite spectacular to observe with a microscope.

If the seed is endospermous, the embryo may be very small, as in the seeds of the buttercup and parsley families. If the seed is a large one, the embryo is usually not difficult to see. For example, pull apart some seeds of castor or morning glory. To do this, peel off the rather tough outer coat and you will find a thin inner coat in the castor seed which is like tissue paper. Peel this off and then gently pry the contents apart along the vertical axis when the two flat, thin, and leafy cotyledons will be exposed to view (Figure 5). In the morning

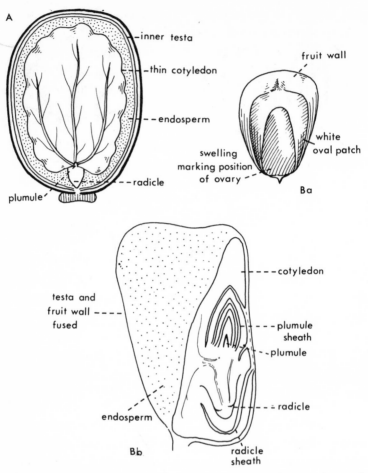

FIGURE 5. *Structure of (A) castor bean, (B,a) corn front view, (B,b) corn longitudinal section*

glory, the cotyledons are folded and their shape is more difficult to make out.

The corn grain shows the general structure that is found in all the grasses. The white oval patch on one side shows the position of the single cotyledon. Look carefully at this and you will see a slight longitudinal swelling running down it. This marks the position of the embryo. Cut the grain longitudinally through the center of this swelling, and examine one half very carefully with a magnifying glass. The embryo is seen to one side of the cut section, partly protected by a cotyledon; the remainder of the grain is filled with a large food reserve. The tiny shoot, or plumule, of the embryo is protected by a plumule sheath, and the radicle by a similar radicle sheath. Although all this is small, it can be seen readily if the grain has been cut in exactly the right plane (Figure 5).

Occasionally seeds contain more than one embryo. Orange and other citrus fruits have seeds with one large embryo and some smaller ones; these you can easily find by dissecting the seeds. Another example is the avocado, one seed of which can produce two or more seedlings. After a time one succeeds at the expense of the other. The food reserve of seeds is all-important for subsequent germination and growth. Small wonder, then, that it is sought after as food by animals of all kinds.

Much of the food reserve is fat or oil. A quick test for fat and oil can be made by rubbing the cut surface of the seed on a piece of brown wrapping paper. A characteristic translucent oily stain is a positive test. Another test for oil involves using a solution of a red dye, Sudan III, in alcohol as an indicator. A very thin slice of the seed should be cut with a single-edged razor blade and soaked in the dye. The dye dissolves in any fat present and colors it red. It is very interesting to examine the slice under the microscope and actually see the oil globules colored red.

It is also possible to crush and boil a number of seeds in water to extract any oil and then test the extract with Sudan III. Another test involves shaking a few slivers of the seed in alcohol, which will dissolve the fat. If this is poured off into cold water, it forms extremely fine droplets, producing a milkiness if fat or oil are present. This is quite a sensitive test.

In all experiments that call for alcohol, the best type to use is ethyl alcohol (pure grain spirits). Due to local laws, ethyl alcohol may be difficult or impossible to get. Isopropyl alcohol, commonly sold as rubbing alcohol, may be substituted in most cases. Methyl alcohol may also be used in some experiments.

The easiest food reserve to test for is starch, which turns a dark blue or black with iodine solution. Cut a corn grain longitudinally and just smear the surface with iodine solution. You can compare the starch content of many seeds. Table 2 is a suggested way to record your results:

TABLE 2—The food reserves of seeds

| Name | Starch | Protein | Fat |
|------|--------|---------|-----|
| Castor oil, etc. | None | Small amount | Large amount |

Notice the distribution of the substance for which you test: whether they are present uniformly throughout the seed and whether they are present in the plumule and radicle.

Occasionally other food reserves are found in seeds: Sweet corn contains sugar, while the date stores a kind of carbohydrate known as hemicellulose. Seeds contain numerous other substances, some of which are poisonous.

# 4 | Seed Germination and Seedlings

The start of seed growth is called germination, and it is easy enough to germinate many seeds from packages. Soak them in a little water, keep them warm, and off they will go. However, it is worth while making a germination test to see exactly how many do grow. One way to do this is to sow 100 seeds from each package by placing them on some damp blotting paper in a saucer. Count the number that germinate within a few days. It is interesting to try these tests on old packages of seeds and on seeds of plants growing in nature. What do you think you will observe? Seed packers usually include a "germination statement" on the package. This is a statement of what percentage of the seeds can be expected to germinate. See if your results agree with the packer's claims.

When all the seeds germinate at the same time, germination is said to be simultaneous. This happens, as a rule, in cultivated plants because man has selected varieties with this property by growing the plants that come up first in any batch sown. If you carry out germination tests with seed collected from wild plants, you will not often obtain simultaneous germination. More than likely you will find intermittent germination over a long period. Sometimes seed germinates better in the second year after sowing, and this you can find out only if you have the patience to grow plants to maturity, collect and store the seeds, and replant a year later. In recording germination, daily counts of the number that grow each day should be made, and the results recorded in a table.

There are several reasons why seeds do not germinate immediately on sowing. Many require conditions in addition to the three essentials—oxygen, water, and a suitable temperature. For example, some seeds are light sensitive and will germinate in darkness.

Carry out germination tests with as many different kinds of seeds as you have, keeping some sets in the dark and others in the light. Try this kind of experiment under light of various colors to see which is most effective. Lettuce seed of the Grand Rapids variety will not germinate in complete darkness, but after a small dose of red light, moistened seed will germinate. But if the red light is followed by far (infra) red light, the initial red treatment is made ineffective. This is called the red far-red reversibility, and this alternation can be repeated a number of times. The response will be that of the last treatment given.

Many seeds, especially those of the pea family (*Leguminosae*), have very thick coats, and uptake of water is not possible until the coat has been cracked, split, or rotted in some way. Take seeds of lupin, sweet pea, or, best of all, canna, and weigh about 20 of them. Then soak them in water for twenty-four hours. Reweigh them. What do you observe? Then repeat the experiment, but file a nick in each before soaking the seeds.

TABLE 3—The uptake of water by seeds

|  | Percentage increase in weight after soaking for three days | Percentage increase in weight after filing and soaking for three days |
|---|---|---|
| Garden pea | 250 approx. | 250 approx. |
| Canna | 0 | 27 |
| Sweet pea | 116 | 233 |

Can you determine any advantage the observed behavior might give the peas in nature?

Other seeds will not germinate until they have passed through a cold period in the moistened state. Try the effect of soaking some apple seeds, hawthorne stones, and other seeds, putting them in a refrigerator before germinating them, keeping sets as controls, of course. Again, observe and try to determine a biological advantage.

You may wonder why seeds do not germinate in the pulp of a berry, for apparently moisture, oxygen, and a suitable temperature are present. The reason, in many cases, is the presence of inhibitors, substances that stop germination. Quite a number of these substances are known. One is coumarin, and you can easily try the effect of this by adding a 1 percent solution of it to 100 cress seeds on damp blotting paper in a saucer, keeping a control set to which an equivalent amount of water is added. A typical result is shown in Table 4.

TABLE 4—The effect of 1 percent coumarin on the germination of seeds

|  | *Number out of 100 that germinated* | *Number out of 100 that germinated after treatment with 1% coumarin* |
|---|---|---|
| Cress | 95 | 3 |
| Lupin | 40 | 0 |
| Radish | 75 | 1 |
| Statice | 6 | 0 |

The pulp of many fruits has such an effect, and you can devise many experiments for yourself, trying the effects of the juices of berries and fruits on the germination of cress and other seeds. It is believed, too, that not only do fruit juices produce substances that inhibit germination, but that some roots can produce substances that stop the growth of seeds nearby.

The seeds of some parasitic plants will only germinate in the immediate neighborhood of their host, and here it has been shown that the roots of the host produce substances that stimulate the growth of the parasite.

There is an African parasitic plant known as witchweed that is quite a serious pest of grains. If a method of synthesizing the stimulating substance were devised, it could be applied to the soil so as to cause premature germination of the parasite's seeds. They would then die, since the host plants would not be available. In this way a serious parasite might be eliminated.

One of the first steps in germination is the intake of water. This can easily be measured by weighing 50 dry peas and soaking them for twenty-four hours and then weighing them again. You can also measure the increase in volume with a graduate cylinder or a measuring cup.

The uptake of water causes formidable pressures. Try filling a plastic bottle or a can to a marked level with dry peas and then adding water. After twenty-four hours find the weight required to squeeze them back to their original level.

How does the water get into the seed? Sometimes it gets through a small hole in the testa, called the micropyle. You can find this in a bean just above the scar of attachment in a bean. In a runner bean the micropyle is at one end of the hilum and there are two tiny swellings at the other end. The micropyle can be stopped up with glue. Soak about twenty beans with stopped-up micropyles in water and compare the water uptake with an equal number of normal beans by weighing them before and after soaking. See Table 5 for typical results.

TABLE 5—The effect of stopping up the micropyles of runner beans on the water uptake

|  | micropyle stopped up | micropyle normal |
|---|---|---|
| Weight of beans | 8.21 gm | 6.37 gm |
| Weight after soaking 24 hours | 14.88 gm | 17.21 gm |
| Percentage increase | 80% | 140% |

Following and coincident with the uptake of water is the

mobilization of the food reserve for use by the growing plumule and radicle. Starch is present in the cells as a tiny grain, and it cannot move about the plant as such; in fact, most food reserves are immobile in the plant. To use them, they must be made soluble in water, and this involves chemical changes. In living organisms these chemical changes are brought about by enzymes which act as catalysts. Starch, for example, is turned to sugar by the enzyme diastase.

To show the action of diastase, germinate some barley grains for about a week till the radicles are just visible. Take a small handful, cover them with water and pound them thoroughly. Here a mortar and pestle are useful, but it can be done with a large spoon and a bowl. Then filter the liquid through a filter paper; the filtrate will contain the enzyme extract.

For filtering, you will need a funnel, filter paper, and something to support the funnel. A ring stand and ring is usually used, but anything, even your hand, will do if a ring stand is not available. Don't forget to place a container under the funnel stem to collect what is filtered.

Fold the filter paper in half. Then fold again at right angles to the first fold.

Open the layers of the fold to form a cone. Place the pointed end of the cone in the funnel. The cone will tend to stay in place in the funnel if the tip of the cone is wet a little bit.

To filter, slowly pour the liquid into the funnel. Do not overfill. It frequently goes rather slowly, so have patience. The liquid that goes through is called the *filtrate*. The material left in the filter paper is the *precipitate*.

Prepare a dilute solution of starch by mixing about a teaspoonful of starch with enough water to make a smooth paste. Then add about 6 ounces of hot water, stirring vigorously. Or you can directly dissolve about a tablespoonful of water-soluble flour in about 6 ounces of water.

Divide the starch solution into two equal portions, in two suitable glass containers. Test tubes are best, but small jars or medicine vials will do. To one container add some of the enzyme extract, and to the other add an equal quantity of water. Let the containers stand for about fifteen minutes, then add a few drops of iodine solution to each. What do you observe? Can you explain your results?

If you have any Fehlings' or Benedict's solution and a source of heat such as a bunsen burner, alcohol lamp, or a gas stove, you can test for sugar in the enzyme-starch sample. You will have to make a fresh preparation, since the iodine will obscure the characteristic color change of the Fehlings' test.

Prepare a starch-enzyme mixture and allow to stand fifteen minutes as before. Fill a test tube to about half capacity with Fehlings' or Benedict's solution. Add a little of the starch-enzyme mixture and heat to boiling. Be sure to use a test-tube holder, and hold the mouth of the tube away from your face. Look for a color change from green, to yellow, to orange. The color change is indicative of the presence of simple sugars (6-carbon sugars). Table sugar, which is not a simple sugar, will not give this result.

The cotyledons (seed leaves) can behave in two ways when a seed germinates; they can remain below the ground all the time or they can come above the ground. The first type is known as *hypogeal* and the second as *epigeal*. This difference can occur in closely related plants. Thus, the runner bean has the cotyledons below the ground while in the kidney bean they come above the ground. We have also seen that the flowering plants can have either one or two cotyledons, and that all seeds may or may not be endospermous. We have, therefore, the following rather complicated set of possibilities:

*Monocotyledons*

1. Epigeal    (a)    endospermous; e.g., onion
                (b)    non-endospermous; e.g., water plantain (*Alisma*)
2. Hypogeal (a)    endospermous; e.g., corn, date or coconut
                (b)    non-endospermous (very rare) cape pondweed (*Aponogeton*) only

*Dicotyledons*
1. Epigeal   (a)   endospermous; e.g., castor, morning glory
          (b)   non-endospermous; e.g., cress, marrow
2. Hypogeal   (a)   endospermous (very rare); e.g., custard apple (*Annona*)
          (b)   non-endospermous; e.g., garden nasturtium

Some of these types of seed can be easily obtained. Of the endospermous monocotyledons with an epigeal type of germination, onion is always available and is easy to grow. The little black seed, if soaked, can be cut and examined with a hand lens, and the embryo will be seen coiled up in a mass of endosperm.

The seeds germinate readily enough on damp blotting paper in a saucer, and the radicle is the first part seen to emerge. This anchors itself in the ground and shortly afterwards tiny lateral roots are formed. The cotyledon, which at first is difficult to distinguish from the radicle, now lengthens, but the tip remains embedded in the seed, and so the whole structure is gradually pulled above the surface of the ground.

The cotyledon turns green and functions as a normal leaf, absorbing carbon dioxide from the air and thus carrying out photosynthesis. This change in color helps to distinguish it from the radicle. The cotyledon also functions as an absorptive organ since the tip serves to absorb the food from the endosperm in the seed and pass it on to the growing tissues (Figure 6).

It is not so easy to find a monocotyledonous seed that is non-endospermous and that has epigeal germination, although it occurs in a group, many of which are water plants. The best known is the water plantain. You can look for it along the sides of streams, ponds and rivers, collect its seed and try to grow it in the following season. The seeds do show a considerable dormancy, but abrading and chipping the seed coat may stimulate germination (Figure 7).

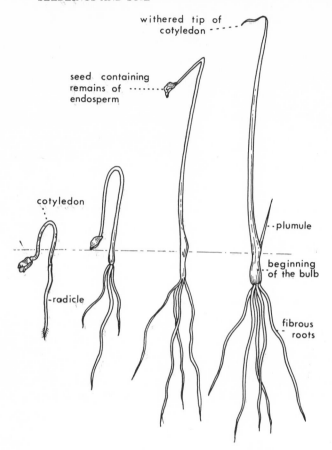

FIGURE 6.  *Germination of the onion.*

All the members of the grass family are endospermous and show hypogeal germination. Corn is an excellent example, particularly the larger fruited varieties. When it germinates— and it is easy to grow—the first part to come above ground is the hard white pointed plumule sheath. This is a hard tube through which the first leaf grows and unfolds (Figure 8). This is an interesting example of one of the ways in which the delicate growing point is protected. During the whole time of germination of the corn the cotyledon remains below the ground and serves to absorb the food reserve from the endosperm and to pass it to the growing root and shoot.

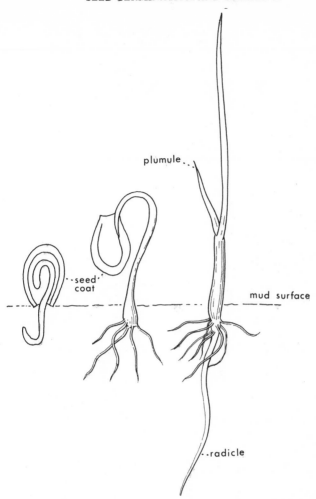

FIGURE 7.   *Germination of the water plantain.*

Another large family of flowering plants with a rather similar pattern of germination is the palm family. Stones (seeds) of the date can be germinated quite readily in a really hot place, say on a radiator. The mass of the stone is a very tough endosperm consisting largely of a material known as hemicellulose laid down as a thickening to the cell walls. The embryo is small and centrally placed. When germination starts, the tip of the cotyledon enlarges to a large mushroom-like mass which invades, dissolves, and absorbs the endosperm and

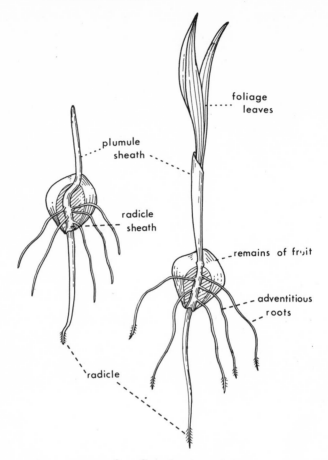

FIGURE 8.   *Germination of corn.*

passes it along a stalk or middle piece to the other end of the
cotyledon which surrounds the developing shoot (plumule).
The extension in length of the middle piece forces the shoot
outside the seed where it is in a position to reach the soil surface.

   The coconut is basically similar. As it usually is seen in
produce stands, it is a one-seeded fruit. The seed is enclosed
by the very thick woody shell. There are three depressions
at one end of the shell that form a "face"-like pattern. One of
the three depressions is thin enough for the seedling to force
its way out. The embryo is small, and the white of the coconut

together with the milk make up the endosperm. In this seed the cotyledon enlarges to a mass as big as an orange, and it absorbs all the nutrients for the growing shoot to use. The food reserve may last for several years so that the absorbing end of the cotyledon remains active for a long time (Figure 9). The middle piece is quite long so that the actual seedling may be some distance from the nut. It is not too difficult to germinate a coconut provided the space necessary in a well-heated greenhouse can be found. It may be necessary to try more than one for, like all other seeds, not every one is viable.

This leaves only one group of monocotyledonous seeds to be mentioned; namely, those that are hypogeal and non-endospermous. This combination is a very rare one and it is known only in one genus, *Aponogeton*. There are several species, and as mentioned before the most common is the cape pondweed (*A. distachyus*). The flowers are white with black anthers and have a scent reminiscent of hawthorn.

Seed is relatively difficult to come by, but if you do manage to obtain any, it must be germinated on mud in shallow water. In this seed the cotyledon is a conical structure with the

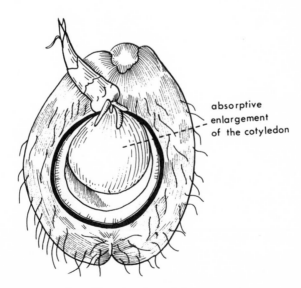

absorptive
enlargement
of the cotyledon

FIGURE 9.   *Germination of the coconut.*

embryo to one side and enclosed in the seed coat. The whole seed floats away from the plant, the seed coat bursts, the contents fall out and sink into the mud where germination takes place. The cotyledon supplies the food material to the shoot at its base which gives rise to the leaves of the new plant (Figure 10).

Turning to the dicotyledons with epigeal germination, we are on far more familiar ground and there are many to choose from. The castor bean and morning glory are good examples. Both of these are easy to find and fairly easily grown, although the castor bean sometimes germinates badly. In the castor bean the radicle emerges and anchors itself in the ground, and then, by subsequent growth of the part away from the tip, the whole seed, testa, and all, is carried above the soil surface. Since it is quite a large seed, it breaks the surface like a miniature earthquake. The cotyledons function for a time as absorbing organs, passing on the food reserve to the

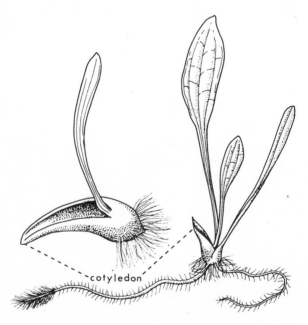

FIGURE 10.    *Germination of the cape pondweed.*

growing point, but later the seed coat drops away and the cotyledons unfold to serve as the two first green leaves. These are more or less oval in shape, whereas the mature leaves are lobed and pointed (Figure 11).

In the morning glory the endosperm is jelly-like and the embryo large, but the seed germinates in much the same way as the castor bean. Here the cotyledons are lobed, almost butterfly-like. Usually the shape of the cotyledons is simpler than that of the mature leaves and in fact cotyledons do tend to look a bit alike. This may be related to the uniformity of their

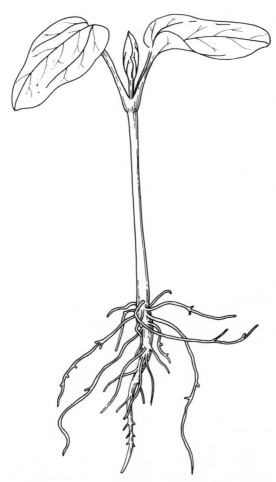

FIGURE 11.   *Germination of the castor bean.*

environment and their similarity in function. However, this is
not completely true, for in some species of the genus *Ipomoea*,
which includes the morning glory, the cotyledons are lobed in
various ways, whereas the adult leaves are heart-shaped. In
the buttercup family the cotyledons are often pointed. In the
parsleys and carrots they are somewhat elongated, despite the
finely divided mature leaves, while in Eschscholtzia (Cali-
fornia poppy) they are forked in a characteristic manner
(Figure 12).

Eschscholtzia is an example of a non-endospermous dicot-

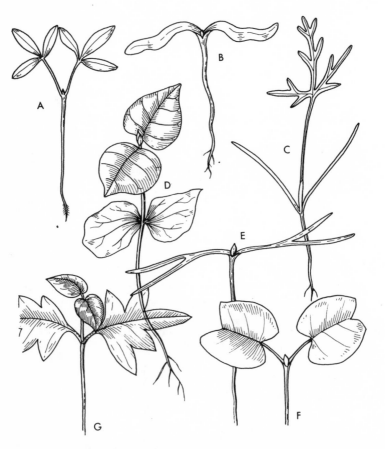

FIGURE 12.   *Cotyledon shapes of some seedlings* (*A*) *cress,* (*B*)
*sycamore,* (*C*) *fennel,* (*D*) *beech,* (*E*) Eschscholtzia californica,
(*F*) Ipomoea purpurea, (*G*) *lyme.*

yledonous plant with an epigeal germination. Other examples include very familiar plants like mustard, radish, and
cress, in which all the food material is packed in the cotyledons. In these seeds the cotyledons tend to remain within the
testa until almost all the food is exhausted. Some of these
have cotyledons with unusual shapes. Cress, for example, has
three-lobed cotyledons. Other seeds that come into this group
are those of marrow, squash, and cucumber. The seeds are
flat and the radicle has a small projection on its inner side
which catches the lower edge of the testa. The elongation of
the plumule above this forces the upper half of the testa to
split and thus aid the emergence of the plumule. This can
easily be seen in any germinating sample of this seed (Figure
13).

Finally, there is a class of endospermous, dicotyledonous
seeds with a hypogeal type of germination. This group is
very uncommon and the members are all tropical plants. One

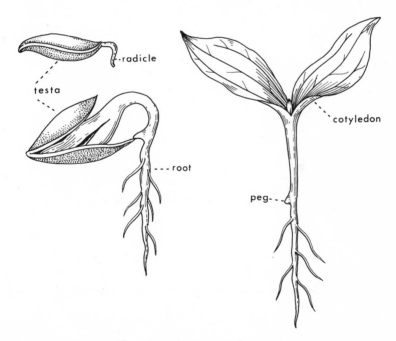

FIGURE 13.  *Germination of the marrow.*

is the rubber tree and the others include the custard apple, the soursop and the sweetsop, all species of *Annona* (Figure 14). Endospermous seeds with hypogeal germination are common in the monocotyledons, rare in the dicotyledons, while the reverse is true of non-endospermous seeds with hypogeal germination.

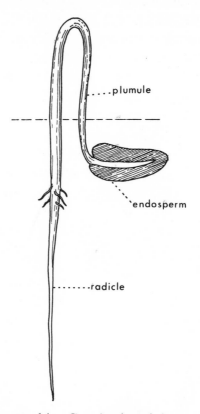

FIGURE 14.    *Germination of Annona.*

# 5 | Transplant Experiments

There are many ways of propagating plants, of making two or more grow where before there was but one. For example, you can propagate by cuttings, by offsets, by grafts, and you can grow new plants from seeds. There is a fundamental difference between the last and the previous methods in that seeds are the product of a sexual reproductive process, and each seed gives rise to a new individual. In the others, a new individual is not produced, but merely a piece of the original is rooted.

When you strike a geranium cutting you take a piece of stem and shoot, stick it into the ground, and it develops roots. Many of the well-known varieties of fruit do not produce viable seeds, and cutting and grafting techniques are the only way to produce new trees. In other instances, seeds will germinate but not grow into the same variety as the parent plants. The same is true for hundreds of our garden plants. Such varieties are called *clones* and the derived pieces are *ramets* of the clone. The great advantage of this method of propagation from the gardener's point of view is that all the plants are alike. Thus, he can plant a flower bed with a single variety and expect all the plants to be similar in shape, and to flower at the same time.

Most of the plants mentioned in the previous chapters come

true from seed. That is, they will grow into the same variety as the parent plant. They have been selected for this property, and the packer guarantees that the color of flower seen on the package is what you will get. Nature is not always so selective, and very close observation of a group of wild flowers will often reveal differences between one individual and another. Planting wild seed gathered from a plant that bore white flowers, for example, will not necessarily produce plants that bear white flowers. We have seen, too, in previous experiments, how the growth of a plant can be altered by the treatment (water, fertilizer, etc.) it receives. Any individual plant is the product of its heredity and its environment, and both affect the final result.

How are the effects of heredity and environment controlled? In previous experiments use was made of carefully selected varieties of seeds, and it was assumed that they were all the same in their inherited make-up. Ramets of a clone are alike in their inheritance, and by growing them in different environments we can see the effect of the environment acting alone. An easy way to do this is to take a large clone of daisy or plantain and to divide it up into a number of ramets as equal in size as possible. Plant half in, say, a sandy soil and the other half in a different soil of your own choice. Devise a method to compare the growth of the two sets of plants. Count the number of fully expanded leaves, the number of flowering spikes, measure the diameter of the rosettes, the height of the plants, and note the duration of the flowering season. If you carry this out carefully, you will find some kinds of plants show great changes in size, etc., in response to different conditions while others do not. It can be interesting, if you have the patience, to grow some of the seeds of daisies or plantains in as uniform conditions as you can, and measure the variation in the resulting individuals.

# 6 | A Little Ecology

Ecology is the study of the relationship of living things to their environment. In recent years the term ecology has been used to describe concern over matters such as pollution and related problems. But to a biologist, ecology is the study of the natural state of environment as well as those problems brought about by man. The plant ecologist is concerned with why certain plants grow only in particular areas, and the interactions of the plants with other living things and their physical surroundings.

There are many ways to carry out investigations in plant ecology. Such investigations can be as casual or as complex as you care to make them. City environments provide as many opportunities for ecological investigations as woods, fields, and mountains.

For a casual study, you can compare the vegetation growing at a roadside with that farther back from the road. Observe the plant growth at a seashore, pond, river, or lake and note how it changes as you move away from the shore. Observe the plants that grow in a cleared lot over an extended period of time. Note the types of plants that grow in cracks in the sidewalk or against the walls of buildings.

In order to carry out a systematic survey, you should designate a specific area. The area can be as large as an entire nation or as small or smaller than cracks in a sidewalk. For obvious reasons, the area you choose for your beginning efforts should not be too large. The size of the study zone depends upon the nature and size of the plants. If the plants are trees, the area of study is necessarily larger than if the predominant plants are mosses. For small plants you could designate a square yard or two, and for larger plants, you could rough out an area of an acre or so, using landmarks such as stones as limiting markers.

Identify whatever organisms you can in the field. Designate unknown plants with a number or letter and take a sample home with you. Try to identify them with the aid of classification keys, a few of which are listed in the Bibliography. Grasses are particularly difficult to identify so it is a good idea to save them until you have gained experience with other plants.

Make lists of plants found in different places. Compare them and you may find that some environments support a wide variety of plants, while others may support only one kind of plant.

There are more ways of studying the relationships of plants to their environment. One interesting thing to do, if you live in hilly country, is to walk up a hillside, noting the changes in the vegetation as you climb. You can stop every 100 yards and make a note of the dominant plants. There may be woodland or plowed land near the base, followed by upland pastures, and, if the mountain is high enough, some truly mountain vegetation near the summit. The causes of the differences you observe are quite complex. Man and animals, climate and soil are interacting factors. Climate is obviously different at the top of a mountain than it is at the bottom. Exposure is much greater, but this is difficult to measure. Wind velocity might be estimated, while humidity and temperature can be measured at a given time.

Long-range investigations will, of course, yield more information than an effort of a day or two. Compare the amount of ground growth in wooded areas in the early spring before the trees are fully foliated with the ground growth after the trees have leaves. If you find plants that grow both in wooded areas and in open fields, compare the rate of growth. Relate your findings.

Estimate, or count if you can, the number of individuals of each species. Determine which species is most numerous and, therefore, is the *ecological dominant* of the area. Note if the plants are crowded together or spread out.

Another investigation you can carry out is a comparison of the plant life in woody, shaded areas and open meadows or roadsides. In addition to taking plant counts, measure as many of the physical factors such as temperature, humidity, and light intensity, as the equipment you have will permit. A thermometer for temperature is obvious. Light intensity

TABLE 6—Light intensity and evaporation in woodlands

| Date | Open | Spruce plantation | Light intensity oak-ash wood | Oak-ash coppice |
|---|---|---|---|---|
| March 13 | 100* | 8 | 71 | 60 |
| May 2 | 100 | 7 | 25 | 18 |
| July 7 | 100 | 5 | 12 | 8 |
| | | Evaporating power of the atmosphere (measured with a simple atmometer) | | |
| May 13 | 100 | 64 | 40 | |
| May 20 | 100 | 61 | 40 | |
| July 7 | 100 | 34 | 18 | |

* Numerals are exposure meter readings.

can be measured with a photographic light meter. A hygrometer or sling psychrometer to measure humidity is an item less likely to be found around the house than a thermometer or light meter. However, humidity measuring devices are readily available and simple ones are not too expensive. Table 6 includes examples of the kind of data that can be gathered in this kind of investigation.

The seashore is a place everyone likes to visit and obviously it has its own special flora, whether it be salt marsh, sand dune, or cliff. Sand dunes are exposed, consisting of fine particles that are easily blown about, and they are near salt water. Plants that grow in such places must be specially adapted to survive in this environment. Marram or beach grass is an abundant grass of sand dunes, and its growth usually keeps pace with the accumulation of sand around its base. Examine carefully a marram plant and dig down through the sand of the dune. You will be lucky if you are able to find the beginning of its root system. Other plants can be explored in the same way.

Other changes occur as dunes get older. Young (or yellow) dunes near the shore have a number of plants on them that are not found on the older (or gray) dunes further from the sea. In fact, the flora of the dunes changes a great deal from young to old dunes, and you can compare the two by making lists. One of the factors with which the change is associated is the acidity of the sand. Sand dunes near the sea are calcareous because of the accumulation of calcium carbonate from the shells of sea animals. As the dunes age, the carbonate is slowly removed and the dune becomes more acid. This can be shown in a simple experiment. Collect samples of sand at intervals as you walk inland over the dunes. Collect the same amount of sand at each interval. Small plastic bags are useful for storing your samples. At home, transfer the sand samples to a suitable glass container and add a little dilute hydrochloric acid to each and compare the fizzing of each sample. Try to assess it on, say, a scale of 0 to 5. The amount of fizzing is roughly proportional to the amount of calcium carbonate present.

Calcium carbonate, of course, is not the only factor responsible for the changes in the vegetation from the young to the old dune. There are many other changes in the soil, as well as subtle differences in the climate and topography.

# 7 | The Work
of Flowers

To most people the flower is the most important and the most attractive part of the plant. Many people refer to flowering plants simply as "flowers." But the flower is only one part of the plant, albeit an important one. It is the reproduction structure of the plant in which seeds are produced. There are many variations in flowers and no flower can be described as typical. But you can get a pretty good idea of flower structure by examining a fairly large flower. You will usually find a set of green outer parts which protect the more delicate parts while in the bud. These are called the *sepals* and all together make up the *calyx*. Then there are the *petals,* often brilliantly colored, which attract the insects for pollination, and are collectively known as the *corolla*. Inside these there are the really essential parts—the stamens which produce the pollen. The pollen gives rise to the male element in the sexual process. In the center of the flower are the female reproductive parts. There is the pistil, bearing at the tip the stigma which receives the pollen. At the lower end of the pistil is the ovary in which the seeds are produced. There is usually a stemlike structure, the style, between the stigma and the ovary.

There are endless variations on this basic pattern; in wind-pollinated flowers, insects are not attracted and the flowers

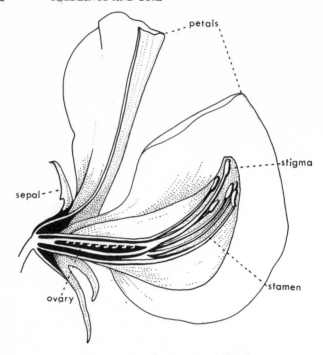

FIGURE 15. *Structure of the flower.*

are inconspicuous, lacing any large bright petals. In some flowers only one set of sexual parts is present; thus flowers may bear stamens only and are said to be male, while in others only the pistil is present and the flowers are said to be female. These kinds of flowers may be borne on the same plant or on different plants. Hazel and oaks have the two kinds of flower on the same tree, but willows, poplars, and hollies have the male flowers on one tree and the females on another. This explains, incidentally, why some holly trees never bear any berries.

Usually, for seed to be formed, the pollen must be transferred to the stigma. This is called pollination and it is brought about by several agencies, the chief being wind or insects. When the pollen grains arrive on the stigma they grow a tube that penetrates down to one or more structures within the ovary called *ovules* which it enters. Within the ovules are the *egg nucleus* and several other nuclei. Here, the main event is a sexual fusion between a *sperm nucleus* and the egg nucleus to form a seed. Each ovule represents one seed. Pollen from one kind of flower will normally germinate on a stigma of the same kind of flower, although occasionally it will grow on the stigma of a closely related flower, and a hybrid between the two may be produced.

It is possible to investigate many aspects of pollination. Open the buds of some flowers very carefully and remove the stamens with a pair of tweezers, taking great care not to burst them, for this will release the pollen in the flowers and spoil the experiment. Allow some of the flowers to unfold and enclose the others in plastic bags to prevent unwanted pollen from reaching the flowers. These flowers will not form seed, but the others, being accessible to insects, will mostly form seed. For this experiment it is well to use a plant with a fairly large flower, from which it is possible to remove the stamens without doing great damage. It is just possible that some of the bagged flowers without stamens will form seed even though no pollen has reached the stigmas and no sexual process has taken place.

There are a number of plants in which the sexual process has degenerated and which are able to form seeds without it. Dandelion is such a plant. With a single-edged razor blade slice off the top of the flower head in the bud just above the level of the tiny fruits. In this way the tops of the stamens and stigmas are removed, and though fertilization is impossible, seed will be formed. This operation is a little difficult because you can cut too low, but a little practice helps. The resulting flower head must be kept moist by being enclosed or covered and should be kept in the shade. You can test the seed for germination very soon after it has formed. This abnormal method of seed formation is called *apomixis,* and it is not so very uncommon in the flowering plants.

Plants have evolved devices to prevent self-pollination, that is pollination of a flower by its own pollen. If a flower bud is tied up in a bag, as previously described, so that insects cannot reach it, it may self-pollinate and form seed. Self-pollination can easily be tested for by tying a number of flower buds in bags and comparing the seed formed with

TABLE 7—The result of removing the stamens
and the bagging of flowers

| Name | Number of flowers from which stamens were removed | Number setting seed |
|---|---|---|
| Wallflower | 48 | 0 |
| Sweet pea | 8 | 0 |
| Everlasting pea | 10 | 0 |
| Canterbury bell | 24 | 0 |
| Foxglove | 9 | 0 |

The result of bagging flowers without removing the stamens

| | Number bagged | Number setting seed |
|---|---|---|
| Everlasting pea | 19 | 0 |
| Sweet pea | 12 | 12 |
| Canterbury bell | 7 | 0 |
| Garden nasturtium | 9 | 9 |

that in flowers without bags. If possible, count the number of seeds formed in the bagged and unbagged flowers. If there are too many and too small to count, they may be weighed if a sufficiently sensitive balance is available. Table 7 shows some typical results.

Cross-pollination tends to improve the vitality of plants by mixing hereditary traits from different individuals. In general, evolution is speeded up by sexual reproduction.

There are many devices by which self-pollination and fertilization are avoided in flowers. In some the stamens ripen so much in advance of the pistils that they have shriveled before the pistils are receptive. The reverse arrangement is also found, in which the stigmas ripen first, although it is not so common as the former. One of the most remarkable ways by which self-pollination is avoided is through *self-incompatibility*. That is, pollen is unable to grow on its own stigma. In this case a bagged flower may self-pollinate, but no seed is formed. This happens in a number of plants, including the garden petunia, and it can usually be demonstrated by bagging some flowers in the bud stage.

Most of the experiments and observations described in this chapter are best carried out on insect-pollinated flowers, since these are usually larger and easier to handle than the smaller wind-pollinated flowers. Insects are attracted by the color and the scent. You can show this, if you have the patience, by removing the petals from some flowers and actually watching and recording the number of insect visits to the flowers with petals and those without.

# 8 | Fruit and Seed Dispersal

Seeds and fruits are spread about the world in many ways. Some of the most effectively spread plants are almost too familiar, like the burrs that have to be pulled one by one from clothing or the masses of winged fruits of elm and sycamore that block the gutters of the streets. While it is obvious that many devices, such as wings, plumes, and hooks, do spread plants about the earth's surface, it is not so well known how far they travel or how efficient one mechanism is compared with another. If you are adventurous and have a ladder you can try spot painting about 100 winged fruits on a sycamore or elm tree and then try to find them after they have been blown from the tree. This experiment is easier if an isolated tree can be found.

An easy way to compare the effectiveness of these mechanisms is to drop the winged fruits of, say, sycamore and ash from the top of a building and see how long it takes for them to reach the ground. The longer they remain afloat, the greater the distance they are likely to be carried. You can try not only with the heavier winged fruits like ash and others but also with the very light-plumed fruits of thistle and dandelion. Since some of these will remain airborne in breezes as light as one mile per hour, you will do better to try the experiment indoors where the air is still.

In wet and damp weather many of the plumed fruits, like those of dandelion, close up, and this means that if they are in the air at the time, they fall to the ground when conditions are favorable for development. Try placing some of these tiny parachutes in water to see if they are easily wetted. Try also the effect of covering an expanded dandelion head with a jelly jar that has been moistened on the inside.

Other fruits have hooks of various kinds that adhere to animals' coats. The burdock, beggar ticks, and cockleburs are well-known examples. You can make a rough comparison of the efficiency with which these burrs cling by hanging up a blanket and throwing the fruits at them, noting the number that cling to the surface and the number that fall to the ground.

Other fruits are dispersed by being eaten by animals, particularly birds. In this case, the fleshy material of the berries is digested by the bird, but the hard seed passes through relatively unchanged. Where birds eat grains, some of the seeds pass through without being digested. You can look at the ground under trees where you have seen birds roosting regularly night after night and see what seedlings are coming up or what plants have grown there. Elder and blackberry are very likely plants to be found.

Some plants have a so-called mechanical means of dispersal, and in these the fruits break open violently and scatter the seeds. This happens in many of the pea family, in the violets and pansies, and in the plants known, for this very reason, as touch-me-nots. You can easily investigate this by getting some pods of gorse and placing them on the floor of an empty room. As they dry, "popping" sounds are sometimes heard and the seeds are thrown several feet. If possible, spread the floor with white paper so you can find the seeds and measure the exact distance they have been thrown. Examine also the way the halves of the pod have twisted up and try to work out how this has scattered the seeds. In the cranesbills each of the five seeds is enclosed in a little case attached to a long and elastic strip of tissue. When this swings upwards the seeds are thrown out. If you can find a specimen, test it by supporting it in a vertical position in the center of a room. The seeds can be thrown in all directions.

Plant tissue that bends or twists according to the moisture content of the atmosphere is adapted for another function. In storksbills, which are closely related to the cranesbills, each of the one-seeded tiny fruits has long spiral, armlike structures that twist and untwist according to the moisture in the air and tend to bury the seeds in the soil. If you can find any of these fruits (and they are not at all uncommon), place a few of them seed end downwards on damp cotton. You can also try them on the surface of fairly loose soil, which you must water from time to time. Wild oats also do the same thing and so, to some extent, do the garden geraniums.

Some plants growing in water, or by the side of water, have their seeds dispersed by water currents. Usually the seeds of fruits float for a time after which they sink into the mud below the surface of the water and germinate. You can collect a number of fruits or seeds of such plants and put them in water and see how long it is before they sink. It may be days or months. Water lilies are good examples. The seeds float until the outer part of the seed coat becomes waterlogged. Water iris is another plant to try.

Other seeds, like those of the rushes (*Juncus*), usually sink immediately or very shortly after contact with water. Later they rise to the surface and begin to germinate and are dispersed as floating seedlings. There are many opportunities for simple experiment here. Try comparing the behavior of the seeds of the various kinds of waterside plants. And, if you can, compare the behavior of a waterside plant with the behavior of a closely related plant that does not grow by the water.

Man, through his activities, is perhaps the most important seed disperser of all. Through trade and commerce millions of seeds of plants are inadvertently carried all over the world.

In a modest way, every individual carries seeds on his own person. Try brushing out your pants cuffs and sowing the dust on damp blotting paper in a saucer. You may be surprised at the number of seedlings that appear. You could also try brushing the mud from a pair of shoes in the same way. Or go one stage further and try a similar experiment with the dirt from under the fenders of an automobile.

There is yet another way of studying dispersal of seeds and fruits; that is by seeing how many plants can reach special sites. For example, make a list of the plants growing on the tops of old walls and try to decide by what method they may have got there. Try to find the nearest individual on the ground from which the seed may have traveled to reach the top of the wall. Of course, quite a lot of seeds may have reached the top of the wall but may have been unable to grow there, so dispersal is not the only factor concerned in determining the flora.

# 9 | Genetics and Plant Breeding

Everyone knows that many of the characters of an organism are passed to its offspring; in fact, this is what is meant when we say, for example, that flower color is inherited. If you buy seeds of the variety of sweet pea known as Gigantic, it is expected that all the flowers will be white, as indeed they are. But we do know of plants that produce seeds that do not breed true to their parents but show a range of colors. This is not an accident but is determined by the laws of inheritance.

These laws were first discovered by an Austrian monk named Gregor Mendel, and he worked with the common garden pea. This is still a suitable plant to work with and if you have the time, patience, and a little piece of ground to use for a garden, you can repeat Mendel's experiments. At least one growing season, essentially a summer, is needed. More summers would be needed to complete all of Mendel's experiments. Mendel worked eight years to gather his data, but you could complete at least one part of them in a summer. If you don't have a summer of time or a garden, Mendelian laws can be investigated in far less time with the fruit fly (*Drosophila*). There are many books that describe Drosophila experiments (see the Bibliography).

If you do repeat any of Mendel's experiments, you will have the satisfaction of knowing that you have carried out part or all of one of the most significant series of experiments in the history of science.

Obtain the following pea seeds:

Improved Pilot: This has round seeds, yellow cotyledons, is tall growing, and has pointed pods.

Little Marvel: This has wrinkled seeds, blue or green cotyledons, is dwarf growing, and has stumpy pods.

These varieties are not quite the same as Mendel used, but they are more readily available. They will breed true; that is, the offspring will resemble their parents very closely and will differ only according to growing conditions. Mendel grew his plants several years before starting his experiments to make sure they would breed true. The garden pea self-pollinates in the bud before the flower opens, and insect visits are not necessary for seed to be formed.

The first step is, of course, to plant the seeds. Do this in accordance with the suggestions given on the seed package for your specific geographical area. Plant the two varieties in two separate areas. Extend all usual care to your plants, such as fertilizing (if necessary), weeding, application of insecticides, and watering if rainfall is not sufficient. Extend equal care to all your plants as nearly as possible. When the plants have grown to the flower bud stage you will be ready for a rather laborious but important step.

Mendel did not allow the plants to self-pollinate, but crossed one variety with another, and this can be done as follows. Select a bud, and remove any others near it so that it stands alone. Then, with a pair of pointed tweezers, gently fold back the upper petals that cover the central keel of the flower, and hold them down with a finger. Insert the tweezers so as to cut through one side of the inner petals covering the keel and open up this part of the flower to expose the ten stamens. Examine them closely, and if they have already burst and shed their pollen, you must find a bud at an earlier stage and start again. If they have not burst, then remove the stamens with the tweezers, counting them as you go so that you take away all ten. But, of course, you must leave the stigma and style untouched.

It is then necessary to return the petals to their original positions and to protect the flower from contamination by foreign pollen. This can be done by covering the emasculated flower with an inverted plastic or muslin bag and tying the mouth around the stem with thread or fine string. A little cotton may be placed in the mouth of the bag if necessary, to prevent damage to the plant stem when tying. All buds that are not emasculated should be removed. Why? It is a good thing to practice the stamen removal on several buds before actually starting the experiment. The more buds you prepare, the better your results are likely to be.

After two or three days the stigma will be ready to receive pollen from a flower of the other variety. Apply some pollen from the other variety to the stigma with an artist's tiny paint brush. Tie the flower up again in the bag and leave it until the pod begins to form. To gather the pollen, open the buds and see if the stamens have burst. If so, remove some of them and place them in a clean container such as a vial.

When the plants have matured, collect the seeeds and save until next year for sowing. What do you notice about the seeds? Peel away a corner of the seed coat of about a dozen seeds to observe the cotyledon color. You have, after one growing season, demonstrated the first Mendelian law— dominance. These seeds represent the *first filial* generation or $F_1$. (It is desirable to make as many crosses as possible, for many seeds will be damaged by weevils or eaten by birds. In fact, it is a very good idea to net the whole plant against birds.)

The following season, the collected seeds should be sown carefully a considerable distance apart and the flowers allowed to self-pollinate and form seed. Check Appendix I for the expected ratios. Do your ratios approach the expected?

If you have carried things this far, you have demonstrated two more Mendelian laws—segregation and random assortment.

If your enthusiasm for growing peas has not diminished,

you can carry your experiments further to a third and even a fourth season. Try crossing the Improved Pilot with a hybrid plant, that is, one that is produced by the cross of the original varieties chosen for the experiments. You could also try crossing the Little Marvel with a hybrid.

Plant the seeds obtained from the second season in separate plots for each of the four seed types (yellow, round; yellow, wrinkled; green, round; green, wrinkled). Allow them to self-pollinate and gather and count progeny as before.

These procedures are considerably easier than the first, since it is not necessary to remove the stamens. The flowers will be allowed to self-pollinate. However, you must extend care to your plants to ensure as big a harvest as possible. As your plants mature, note the height of the plants and the shape of the pods. Remember that the stems and the pods still represent the First Filial generation, while the seeds in the pods are a new generation, the *Second* Filial generation.

When the plants have matured, break the pods and gather the seeds. Count the number of seeds that are smooth (round) and the number that are wrinkled. Then spot check the number of seeds with yellow cotyledons and those with green cotyledons. Again, the color of the cotyledons can be observed by peeling away enough of the seed coat to see the cotyledons. (Do this with only a few seeds, for you will want to save them for the next series of experiments.)

Determine the following ratios (expressed as 2:1, 3:1, 4:1, etc.)

number of round seeds to wrinkled seeds

number of yellow cotyledons to green cotyledons

Number of round yellow to round green to wrinkled yellow; to wrinkled green

See Appendix I for the notation used to express the crosses and the expected results.

Another good plant to work with is corn. This large grass requires a long and warm summer to do really well, but it can be grown in almost any part of the United States (with the possible exception of Alaska) and southern Canada. In colder areas the grains should be sown early in the spring in a warm greenhouse and planted outside in May. Corn is monoecious, bearing the male flowers in a head or tassel and the female flowers lower down in a cob with the stigmas (silks) protruding from the apex at flowering time. Pollination is by wind. Large amounts of pollen are produced by the male flowers, which is carried to the silks of the female flowers. Hybridizing two varieties is not difficult. All you have to do is to grow the two chosen varieties (say, one with yellow grains and the other with white grains) side by side and remove all the tassels from the white plants as they form. Thus, the only pollen being blown about will be from the yellow, and if it falls on its own stigmas it will give true breeding yellow, but if it pollinates the white the grains will be hybrids. Yellow is dominant to white, so if you take some of the grains from the white plant and sow these side by side, the following year cobs with 3:1 ratio will be obtained. The result may be expressed

Yellow-grained plant v. White-grained plant

(YY)                    (yy)

yellow grains $F_1$

(Yy)

---

1YY      2Yy      1yy

i.e., 3 yellow to 1 white

If you can get a purple- or red-grained variety, you can grow these alongside the white varieties. Then de-tassel the white varieties as soon as the tassels appear so that no pollen is spread from these by the wind. Allow the tassels of the red-grained varieties to flower and you will get cobs on the white plants pollinated by the red and cobs on the red plants pollinated by the red pollen. The results will depend on the exact genetic constitution of the plants concerned. Refer to more advanced books on genetics.

Most, if not all, of the varieties of garden and crop plants have been produced by breeding experiments fundamentally similar to those described here. The range of color in sweet peas, the varieties of the garden flowering plants such as the rose are examples. If you do try further experiments for yourself, do not always expect to obtain such simple ratios as have been given here, for genetics is a very complex subject, and there are many complications to the very simple picture that has been presented. You may wonder how many of the inherited variations have come into being. The short answer is that changes in the heredity mechanism occur spontaneously in nature. Man has found means of speeding up the occurrence of these mutations, as they are called; one way is by exposing seeds to radiation. The effect is to cause a number of usually harmful mutations. Irradiated seeds can be purchased from various mail-order biological supply firms. If you carry out experiments with irradiated seeds, you should also plant normal seed as a control. One of the things to look for in irradiated seed is percentage of germinations.

# 10 | Introductory Plant Physiology and Biochemistry

Some of the earlier experiments in this book indicated that water is the first and most important nutrient for plants. Keep water from a plant and it will not grow at all. It is true, some plants like cacti grow in deserts and survive long periods of drought, but their growth is very slow compared with the typical garden plants.

Plants pass the water through vessels in their roots, stems, and leaves and lose nearly all of it to the atmosphere through their leaves by a special kind of evaporation called transpiration. The amounts of water lost in this way may be quite large. Stephen Hales, one of the earliest plant physiologists, writing in 1727, recorded that a large sunflower plant with a leaf area of thirty-nine square feet gave off about one pint of water in the twelve hours of a hot day while a cabbage with about half this leaf area gave off about one and a quarter pints. Others have estimated that a birch tree might give off about ninety gallons (400 kiloliters) on a sunny day while a really large tree may give off a ton of water per hour.

Some plants exude water from the edges of their leaves in a process known as *guttation*. These plants have water-secreting pores round the leaf edges, usually at the tips of veins, and in early morning, drops of water may be seen at these points. Strawberry plants exhibit this phenomenon. Here again the amounts may be large. The taro or coco (*Colocasia antiquorum*), which is an Indian plant with very large leaves (about a yard and a half long by half a yard wide), has been known to produce 200 ml. (about one-third of a pint) from a single leaf in one day.

One way to show this great water loss is to use paper (filter or white blotting paper) soaked in a 3 percent solution of cobalt chloride. When really dry, this paper has an intense blue color but it changes to a pale pink when it becomes moist. If a strip of blue paper is applied to a leaf surface and held in position for a short length of time, it rapidly becomes pink. The more rapid the loss of water (transpiration) the faster the color change. If strips of this paper are fastened on to the surfaces of leaves and held in position by glass microscope slides (or something similar) a rough comparison of the rates of transpiration can be made by taking the times for the color to change. It is essential that the paper be dry in the first place and that it is rapidly placed in position, for the moisture in the atmosphere soon induces changes (Figure 16).

More elaborate methods exist for measuring this water loss. One is to take a whole plant, roots and all, and place it in a bottle of water. The surface of the water is covered with a

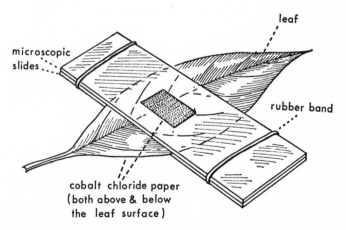

leaf

microscopic slides

rubber band

cobalt chloride paper
(both above & below
the leaf surface)

FIGURE 16.   *The use of cobalt chloride paper.*

little oil to prevent evaporation from this water surface, and the level carefully noted from day to day. As the water is absorbed, so the level falls, and the actual amount may be measured by refilling the bottle up to the original level from a measuring cylinder. This experiment really measures the rate of water uptake by the roots, which is almost the same as the amount lost by the leaves.

The actual path the water follows from the root to the leaf may be seen if a garden weed is dug up, its roots washed free of soil and placed in water colored with red ink or food coloring. In an hour or so the red ink will pass into the plant with the water, coloring the tissue through which it passes. If the root, stem, and leaf are cut across at various places and examined with a lens, the conducting tissue, called *xylem,* will be seen. This tissue is placed mainly centrally in the root, but toward the outer edge of the stem and in the veins of the leaf. Seen under the microscope the xylem consists of fine long tubes with few cross walls, but with strongly thickened side walls. This can also be done with a cut celery stalk. Cut off a piece at the wide end and place the cut end in the colored water.

As seen in previous chapters, plants obtain not only water but mineral salts from the soil. From the air leaves obtain carbon dioxide, and with the aid of light basic carbohydrate molecules are built which are assembled into more complex carbohydrates in the leaf cells. The most important of these is starch, which incidentally, is the most easily detected (see page 22). Starch gives a blackish-blue color in the presence of iodine solution, and it is quite easy to test some parts of plants like tubers, rootstocks, and seeds for starch by cutting them open and smearing the freshly cut surface with iodine solution. Starch is the form of carbohydrate that is stored. You can work through a number of vegetables like potatoes, artichokes, parsnips, or fruits like bananas or seeds like beans in this way. Nearly all contain starch but some plants make storage carbohydrate compounds of a slightly different chemical composition which do not turn blue with iodine.

You can test for starch in leaves if you first remove the chlorophyll so that blue-black color of the iodine test can be observed.

Geranium leaves are an excellent choice for this investigation. For best results, the plant should have been in sunlight for several days. Place the leaves in boiling water for a few minutes. This is to soften the leaves. Then place the leaves in a container such as a beaker that is half-filled with methyl or ethyl alcohol. Heating the alcohol will usually result in the removal of the chlorophyll. How long it takes depends on the thickness of the leaf, but it's generally about five minutes.

It is, however, very dangerous to heat alcohol directly. Place the container of alcohol and leaves in a larger container of water, such as a cooking pot. The level of water should be such that a little more than half of the alcohol container is immersed. Boil the water and the chlorophyll will be removed, but it will take a little longer than direct heating. Be sure you turn off the flame before removing the container of alcohol from the water. Do not discard the alcohol or attempt to retrieve the leaves until the alcohol is completely cooled.

Not all plants store starch in leaves. You can also test for starch and other organic substances in stems, roots, and seeds.

The test for glucose is the Benedict's solution or Fehlings' solution test described on page 28. You can test for glucose in apples by cutting up an apple, boiling a few pieces in sufficient water to cover, and subjecting the water extract to the Benedict's or Fehlings' test. Boil the apple pieces for only a minute or so. Longer boiling may destroy the glucose.

Testing for sucrose (table sugar) is more involved and requires the use of dangerous chemicals. To about 10 ml. of the test solution, which can be sugar water or a plant juice, add one or two drops of 5.0 per cent cobalt nitrate solution (5 grams cobalt nitrate in 100 ml. of water). Then add four or five drops of 50.0 percent sodium hydroxide solution (50 grams sodium hydroxide in 100 ml. of water, or smaller quantities in proportion). A resultant violet color is a positive test for sucrose. The sodium hydroxide is very dangerous to handle, and if you carry out this investigation, use goggles, rubber gloves, and a rubber apron. Sodium hydroxide is sold as pellets or sticks and must be handled with tongs or a spoon. It is suggested that the sucrose test be carried out under the supervision of a teacher or other qualified person.

Plants respond to various stimuli. It is generally known that they "grow toward the light," but really it is only the tips of the main shoots that respond in this way. Roots react differently, being relatively or completely insensitive to light, yet responding to gravity. One of the most exciting responses is shown by plants that are sensitive to touch. The sensitive plant (*Mimosa pudica*) is a very striking example and seed for planting is fairly easy to obtain. It germinates well in a warm place (preferably a greenhouse) and can be grown quite easily. When touched, the leaflets fold up, and ultimately the whole leaf droops. After a lapse of time it recovers and the leaves unfold again.

Take a well-grown and well-watered Mimosa plant and pinch one of the top leaflets with a pair of tweezers. Observe how the leaflet folds up and how the stimulus is passed to nearby leaflets. Note how long it takes for the stimulus to spread. Allow the plant to recover and stimulate it again in the same way and take the time as before. Try to see if there is any evidence of "fatigue" in the response. There are other experiments you can try. See, for example, how the response is affected if the plant is placed in a much cooler situation and try the effect of covering the plants so they are in the dark. It is, by the way, important to avoid jarring the plants when moving them.

Even more exciting is the movement of the Venus's flytrap (*Dionaea muscipula*), a plant that grows in swampy areas in southern United States. It has to be grown in peat, but plants can be bought in nurseries, hobby stores, from mail-order firms, and even in supermarkets. It must not be watered with a hard water.

The leaf blade of this plant is in two halves hinged at the base so that they can close together. The edges of the leaf blade are set with stiff spines, which interlock rather like the teeth of a trap. The inner surface of each part of the leaf has about three long stiff hairs which are exceedingly sensitive. When one is touched, the two halves of the leaf close suddenly. The time taken is about ten to twenty seconds, which is fast enough to trap any insect wandering over the leaf.

One very significant point about these sensitive leaves is that they do not react to water drops falling on the sensitive hairs and remain open during rainfall. They grow in nitrogen-poor soil. What is the significance of this?

If you have a small chemistry set, it is likely to contain many of the chemicals needed for the following experiments. You have already extracted chlorophyll. Now you will separate chlorophyll and other plant pigments from leaves.

Chlorophyll is the substance in plants that enables them to use light energy in the making of carbohydrates. Actually chlorophyll, as extracted from most plants, is a mixture of at least four complex substances. Two of these are the chlorophylls a and b. Chlorophyll a is a blue-black solid that gives a green-blue solution in alcohol, while chlorophyll b is a green-black solid that gives a green solution in alcohol. Two other substances, or rather groups of substances, are present; namely, the *carotenes,* which are orange-red, and the *xanthophylls,* which are yellow.

The pigments can be separated by various techniques of *chromatography.* The general idea is to extract the chlorophyll with a solvent and then allow the chlorophyll-solvent mixture to migrate through various materials such as paper toweling, filter paper, or chalk. When used in this way such materials are called adsorbents. The pigments will migrate through the adsorbent at different rates and separate.

Fresh spinach leaves are a good source of chlorophyll pigments. Cut up two or three spinach leaves as finely as possible and place the cuttings in a mortar or other suitable container. Add enough acetone to just cover the leaf cuttings.

CAUTION: ACETONE IS EXTREMELY FLAMMABLE. THERE MUST NOT BE ANY OPEN FLAMES NEAR YOUR WORK SPACE. BE SURE THE ROOM IS WELL VENTILATED AND AVOID BREATHING THE FUMES.

Grind the leaves until the acetone is a very dark green. If you do not have any acetone, fingernail polish remover is an adequate substitute. These products are usually mostly acetone, but frequently contain an oily substance that may interfere with the results of your experiment.

One of the handiest adsorbents is a piece of white blackboard chalk. Make sure the chalk is trimmed evenly so that it will stand unsupported. Dip one end of a piece of chalk in the chlorophyll extract and allow the end to dry. Repeat the dipping and drying about three or four times. Then stand the stained end of the piece of chalk in a little fresh acetone. In fifteen minutes to an hour, depending on the quality of the chalk, bands of color will separate as the liquid travels up the chalk.

You should see four bands of color. From the top down they are orange-yellow (carotene), yellow (xanthophyll),

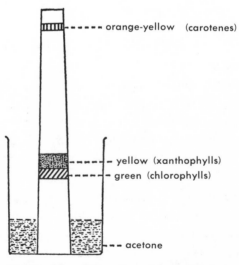

FIGURE 17. *Separation of leaf pigments.*

chlorophyll a, and chlorophyll b. Chlorophyll a is blue-green, and chlorophyll b is yellow-green.

There are many possible combinations of solvent and adsorbent. You can try the following with filter paper or paper toweling. Cut the paper into strips about an inch wide, and preferably pointed at one end. The length of the strips is determined by the height of the container into which you pour the solvent and immerse the strip.

Draw a line in ordinary pencil across the strip near the bottom. With a fine dropper or a stirring rod, place a small drop of the chlorophyll extract at about the mid-point of the line you have drawn. Allow it to dry; repeat three or four times.

Select a glass container, which can be almost anything, such as a test tube, jar, or bottle. The one important requirement is that there must be a means of closing the container. Pour solvent in the container to a depth so that the level of the liquid will be just below the pigment spot. Then cover the container and shake it to saturate the atmosphere in the container. Suspend the strip from the cover so that the strip dips into the solvent. Do not submerge the pigment spot. You can use anything to suspend the strip—tape, staples, or whatever you happen to have. You could also roll a larger piece of paper into a cylinder, staple the edges together, and stand the paper cylinder in the solvent. Allow the strip to remain in the solvent until the pigments separate. This time can be as little as ten minutes.

Try different brands of paper toweling to see which is best. You can also experiment with combinations of different solvents. Unfortunately, the suitable solvents, such as acetone, petroleum ether, formic acid, and acetic acid are dangerous substances. Exercise *extreme* caution in using them. Rubber gloves and a rubber apron should be used. If you have a history of allergy to bee stings, avoid formic acid.

Green plants, as a group, are referred to as *autotrophs.* That is, they make their own organic food from inorganic materials. The food-making process, called *photosynthesis,* is the link between the non-living, inorganic world and the world of living things. Photosynthesis makes life possible for *hetero-trophs,* such as animals, including man, not only because photosynthesis is the ultimate food-producing process, but also because it is the primary source of atmospheric oxygen. Photosynthesis is not the only autotrophic process that occurs on this planet, but it is the major one.

Photosynthesis is a very complicated process, and it is beyond the scope of this book to go into a detailed discussion. Scientists have not yet been able to duplicate photosynthesis in the laboratory, but the process has been minutely studied, and you, too, can investigate certain aspects.

Basically, photosynthesis is the chemical conversion of water and carbon dioxide to organic substances called carbohydrates. The energy for this process is light, and the substance that makes plants green, chlorophyll, traps the light energy and makes it available for the process.

A convenient, but inaccurate and incomplete, way to summarize photosynthesis is with the following chemical equation:

$$6\ CO_2 + 6\ H_2O \xrightarrow[\text{light}]{\text{chlorophyll}} C_6H_{12}O_6 + 6\ O_2$$

carbon+water         six carbon+oxygen
dioxide                sugar
                        (glucose)

Many things happen to the $CO_2$ and $H_2O$ before the primary product, which is not a 6-carbon sugar, is produced. However, the primary product, molecules of a 3-carbon sugar, quickly pair up to form the 6-carbon sugar which is usually glucose. $CO_2$ and $H_2$ are the primary materials that go into the process, and oxygen is one of the products.

The 3-carbon sugar, called phosphoglyceraldehyde (PGAL) can be utilized immediately as food, but it is most frequently converted to glucose for transport to other parts of the plant. From glucose, other more complex carbohydrates are made. Glucose is an example of what is called a single or simple sugar. The term monosaccharide is also used to designate simple sugars. The formula $C_6H_{12}O_6$ can be used to designate other simple sugars such as fructose. What we ordinarily call sugar is a double sugar, sucrose, which can be written as $C_{12}H_{22}O_{11}$. Note that the formula is $C_6H_{12}O_6 \times 2$, but minus one molecule of water ($H_2O$). However, as with glucose, the formula can be for other double sugars or disaccharides. The arrangement of the atoms makes the difference. More complex carbohydrates, called polysaccharides, such as starch and cellulose, are made of many monosaccharide units.

Plants also synthesize proteins and fats. Nitrates absorbed from the soil comprise much of the raw material for protein synthesis.

Although it is not possible for you to duplicate photosynthesis, there are many investigations you can carry out to demonstrate that photosynthesis is going on. You can, as has been discussed, also extract chlorophyll from leaves and you can test for the presence of various food substances.

From an aquarium supply store, you can obtain some *Elodea* (also called *Anacharis*) which is a common pond plant frequently used in aquaria. If *Elodea* is not available, you can use almost any other free-floating aquatic plant. Fill a container, such as a test tube, with water and place a sprig of *Elodea* in it. Place your thumb over the mouth of the test tube and stand the test tube in an inch or two of water in a bowl. When you have finished this operation, the test tube should still be filled or almost filled with water. If not completely filled, mark the level of the water. Repeat the operation with at least one more sprig of *Elodea,* test tube and bowl of water. Place one set-up in a place with light and place the other in darkness. Allow them to remain two or three days. From time to time, observe the plant that is in light. You should be able to see bubbles of gas issuing from the leaves.

After two or three days, compare the level of the water in the tubes. What is the gas in the tubes? If you have collected enough gas, test it by inserting a glowing splint into the tube.

To do this, place your thumb over the mouth of the tube while it is still in the water. Remove the tube, mouth down, remove your thumb and quickly insert the glowing splint. The glowing splint bursting into flame is a positive test for oxygen.

You are well aware that light is necessary for plant growth. However, plants will grow better in some colors of light than in others. To test this, you will need some potted plants such as geraniums, some flood lights, and some colored gelatin or acetate of the type used for theater lighting. The latter may be obtained at theatrical supply stores, or around Christmas time at "seasonal shops" when circles of colored acetate are sold as Christmas tree decorations.

Set up plants, lights, and acetate in separate areas so that you have plants growing in white light, green light, red light, and blue light. Allow the plants to grow for about a week. Measure the plants before and after the experiment. In which color did the plants seem to do best? Observe the appearance of the plants. Note especially the plants that were grown in green light. Can you explain your observations?

Most plant leaves are green, but flowers exhibit a variety of bright colors. Color in flowers is largely caused by compounds called *anthoxanthins* and *anthocyanins*. Anthoxanthins are common in leaves as well as in flowers, and they show a limited color range. These pigments turn a bright yellow when exposed to ammonia vapors. Put a few drops of ammonia in a flask or narrow-neck bottle and through the neck pass a white flower such as a white lily or lilac or almost any other white flower. It will turn yellow, but if dilute acid is put in the flask the yellow color will fade. With a little ferric chloride solution, a green or brown color is produced.

To see if anthoxanthins are present in leaves, make a hot-water extract of any green leaves and carry out the tests described above. Common plants such as dandelion, violet, and plantain all contain anthoxanthins.

Practically all the blue, red, and purple colors of flowers, fruits, and stems are due to anthocyanins. These pigments are found dissolved in the cell sap, and it is an exception to find a plant without them. These can be extracted with alcohol, preferably ethyl. It is best to use flower petals since they have fewer additional substances than leaves. Grind some petals with an 80 percent solution of alcohol, and filter. To the filtrate, add a little dilute acid and notice the bright red color. Add a little dilute alkali (such as ammonia water or a solution of baking soda) to a little of the extract and it will turn green. This shows a property of many of the anthocyanins; namely, that they act as acid-base indicators. Litmus, a widely used acid-base indicator, is derived from the pigments in a lichen.

It follows that if the acidity of the cell sap changes, so will the color of the dissolved anthocyanin change. This is one of the ways in which flower color is altered, as, for example, in some kinds of morning glory where the colors change as the flower opens and fades.

Test the alcohol extract also with a dilute solution of ferric chloride; if the extract is reasonably pure, it will give a slaty-blue to a purple color, but if it contains some anthoxanthin, as is quite likely, it will give a more olive-brown color. Test the extract also with a dilute solution of sodium hydroxide and also with a dilute sodium carbonate solution, and compile a table showing the results. The exact colors obtained will depend on the different anthocyanins and xanthins present in your extracts, which again depends on the flowers you have used. Plants which often give results quite different from the usual include members of the Chenopodiaceae (e.g. beetroot), the Phytolaccaceae (e.g. pokeweed) and the Portulaceae (e.g. purslane). The pigments of these are largely soluble in water, in contrast to those first mentioned which have to be extracted with alcohol.

Substances known as *leuco-anthocyanins* produce anthocyanins on heating with dilute (10 percent) hydrochloric acid. If you can obtain some amyl alcohol try the following. Take a few square centimeters of leaf tissue, chop them very finely, and place them in a test tube. Then cover the leaf tissue with dilute hydrochloric acid, and keep the tube warm for about fifteen to twenty minutes. This can be done by placing the tube in a support in a saucepan of boiling water. After this an equal volume of amyl alcohol is added to each tube, the contents shaken and allowed to settle. CAUTION: DO NOT PUT YOUR THUMB OVER THE TUBE WHEN YOU SHAKE IT. USE A STOPPER. A red color in the amyl alcohol indicates the presence of *anthocyanidin* but a green color, or hardly any color at all, indicates the absence of anthocyanins. A number of different kinds of leaves may be tested in this way. You will find that plants of the same family tend to give similar results, and biochemical investigations are frequently used by plant taxonomists to confirm relationships based on structure.

# 11 | Plant Products

The plant may be compared to a chemical factory producing all sorts of compounds of unending complexity. Just think for a moment of all the compounds we get from plants such as foods of many kinds, flavoring matters of great variety, drugs and medicines, fibers of all sorts, essential oils and scents, and so on. A single plant has a capacity for chemical synthesis which makes man's efforts seem clumsy.

It is often said that bread is the staff of life, so important is it to the diet of the Western world. Bread is made from wheat flour, and if you test either the flour or the grain with iodine you will find it to contain a very large quantity of starch. To make bread, flour is mixed with water and the fungus known as yeast and left to "work" for a time. The yeast produces carbon dioxide which inflates the dough, and when it has finished rising the bread is baked.

This can be shown by an interesting experiment. Take about 5 gm of yeast and make this into a stiff dough with 25 gm of flour (not self-rising) and water. Roll the dough into a short plug on a flat surface and then drop it into an empty measuring cylinder. Any parallel-sided glass or plastic jar will do, but a narrow one is best. If you use a jar, stick a piece of paper down one side, and mark it at equal intervals so as to make a scale (Figure 18). Immediately on placing the

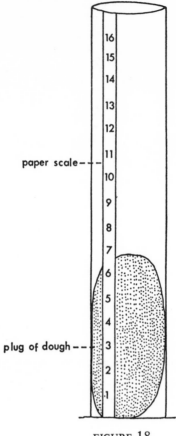

paper scale

plug of dough

FIGURE 18.

dough into the cylinder or jar, read its height, and do this every five minutes for about an hour, or until it does not rise any more. Then press it down again with a spoon or piece of wood, and see what happens in the next half hour.

It is a curious fact that if you try to make a dough with flour from other grains, say for example rice, it will not rise. It is remarkable that you can only make raised bread with rye or wheat flour. Starch is the common ingredient of all these grains, but individually they differ in their protein content. Only rye and wheat have the right kind of protein for bread making. The types of wheat proteins called *glutens* make a sort of elastic mass with water which stretches as the carbon dioxide produced by the yeast bubbles through it. If you make a dough precisely as indicated above and hold it under a running tap, the starch is gradually washed away as a milky liquid and ultimately you are left with a sticky mass of gluten. To wash away all the starch takes a long time, but in fifteen minutes you will notice quite a difference in the dough. It is the presence of gluten that enables bread to be made. Moreover, its amount greatly affects the quality of the bread. Wheat that contains 12 to 14 percent gluten is known as hard wheat, a variety widely grown in North America.

Wheats grown in milder climates, like that of the British Isles, contain less protein and are known as soft wheats. They do not make such good bread and are mainly used for making biscuits.

You can try experimenting with a rather minor plant product and make some writing ink. The earliest inks known to Egyptian and Chinese civilizations about 2500 B.C., were made with lamp black and a solution of a glue or gum. This was usually diluted with water before use. Colored juices of plants were also used, but the blue-black ink in use for many centuries was made from plant tannins and an iron salt. You can make your own writing ink in the following way. Find some of the brown spherical galls that are found on the oak tree— they have various names, "oak gall," "oak apple," "oak marble," "oak nut," "marble gall," and they are usually more frequent on scrub oak and young trees than on older mature trees. Pound them into a powder in a mortar or bowl. Boil the powder with a small amount of water and allow it to stand for a while. Then filter; the filtrate will contain tannin. If a little of this is diluted with water and a drop or two of 5 percent ferric chloride solution is added, a deep blue-black ink is produced. If used for writing on paper, it may be faint to begin with but on standing it becomes darker and insoluble in water. This insolubility gives the ink its permanence, so that it does not wash out when the paper is wetted. Experiment with different concentrations of tannin extract solution.

Many soluble dyes are now used for all kinds of colored

inks. These fade in strong light and wash out in water, and are suitable only when a lasting permanent record is not required. They will, however, last quite a long time if well protected. Ball-point inks also consist of dyes or pigments in oils or resins and are really more like printing inks.

If you can't find any oak galls, you can use the bark stripped from two- to three-year-old twigs of the oak, but it should be cut into small pieces for extraction in boiling water. You can also use the bark of the sumach (*Rhus coriaria*) or the bark of the sweet chestnut. Even the leaves of the latter contain some tannins and can be used. If you use the bark of the horse chestnut and treat the extract with ferric chloride solution, a green color results. Walnut and larch also give this reaction, but it is necessary to boil well to get a sufficient amount of the tannin extracted.

One other interesting point about the horse chestnut may be studied. It contains *aesculin,* a substance that belongs to a group of compounds known as *saponins,* and it gives a remarkably blue fluorescent solution. To observe this, strip the bark from some young twigs and boil them in a little water. Filter and pour the filtrate into a larger amount of water, and the blue fluorescence should be seen.

# 12 | Grafting and Budding

There are many ways of propagating plants other than planting seed; striking cuttings is a familiar method of raising geraniums or chrysanthemums. It has some special advantages for the horticulturist; for one thing, one can be sure that all the plants will be the same, and so a gardener can produce the "carpet bedding" commonly seen in parks and large gardens. Taking cuttings is also particularly valuable for those varieties of plants that do not grow true from seed.

Plants differ greatly in their capacity to root from cuttings. Most willows, especially the pussy willow shoots, will root and grow if pressed into damp ground. It is also quite easy to root a number of shrubs, like fuchsias and roses, but it is very difficult to do the same with apples and pears although they belong to the same family as the rose. Apples, pears, and particularly roses are known in countless varieties, most of which do not grow true from seed. Also, to raise apple trees from seed requires about ten years or more before they will bear fruit, and this is one of the reasons why apples and pears are propagated by grafting. In grafting, a shoot known as a *scion* is shaped and fitted into an incision prepared in the stem of an established, rooted plant called the *stock*. A good contact between the growing tissue of the stock and scion is essential for success, and the two are bound together and covered with a material such as wax so that the tissues do not dry up before they have grown together. By the process of grafting we obtain uniform individuals, just as in the practice of taking cuttings, and further, an apple tree becomes capable of bearing fruit in five years or about half the time it would normally take.

There is one difficulty as far as apples are concerned, and that is the production of a sufficient number of stocks, since cuttings do not root easily. This can be overcome by layering shoots; i.e., covering the basal parts with soil while they are still connected to the parent, but it still takes two years for them to root. Although grafting assures that the variety comes true to form, it has been found that the kind of stock used will greatly affect the growth of the resulting tree.

With patience, you can raise your own apple trees. Various stocks can be bought from nurseries that specialize in fruit trees, and they should be planted out and allowed to establish themselves. Then in the following autumn choose a suitable scion which has the same diameter as the stock and cut as shown in the diagram (Figure 19). The fit between stock and scion should be as close as possible, and the two should be tied together tightly with raffia and the union coated with grafting wax. A good material to use for this and for all grafting is the rubber tape found in the middle of some golf balls. It is quite elastic, it holds stock and scion together, and the loose end can be sealed with a little rubber cement.

As a rule you can only graft varieties of one species on one another; e.g., apples on apples, roses on roses, etc. Sometimes you can graft a species on another very closely related one, but that is usually as far as you can go. You can graft apple on pear, but it will only grow for one or two years during which time it weakens and dies. Lilac is often grafted on privet, but it does not last very well. Sometimes grafting is used to start the plant off as in some delicate varieties of clematis. These are grafted on to small plants of more vigorous species and planted with the graft below soil level. Then the scion produces its own roots and ultimately becomes independent of the original stock.

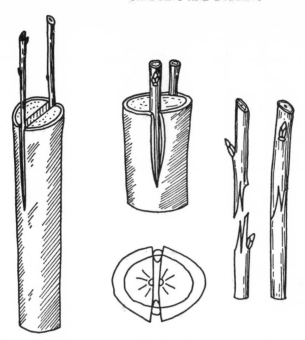

FIGURE 19.   *Grafting techniques.*

Budding is a similar practice; it consists in making a T-shaped insertion in the bark of the tree or shrub and gently opening the cut so that a small segment of the scion bearing a bud can be inserted underneath. This piece must be suitably shaped and must consist only of a piece of bark with a bud so that contact and ultimately union is achieved between stock and scion. After insertion of the scion, the flaps of the bark of the stock are folded over, the whole tied with raffia and waxed over. This increases the chances of contact between the *cambia* (actively growing regions) and lessens the chances of drying out or of infection by disease (Figure 20). Most budding operations are carried out in the summer, and union between the two parts may be achieved in about two weeks. The buds, however, may not grow until the following spring.

Try to do this with roses. You can either buy stocks from a nursery man or collect a few shoots of a wild rose in hedge-

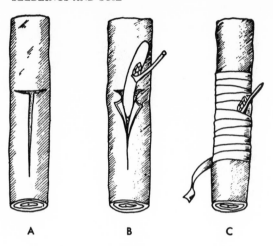

A          B          C

FIGURE 20.  *Budding technique*

rows or on some waste ground. When collecting, remember that each should have some roots, and grow them until well established. Then cut them down almost to ground level and proceed to bud them, as described above and shown in Figure 20, with buds from any of your favorite rose bushes. Insert at least two buds on each stock. Leave the plants for the winter, and in the following spring cut back the stock right to the budded region. This will stimulate the buds to develop. Do not allow any suckers from the stock below the ground to grow. Cut them off below the ground as near to their origin as possible for they compete with the young developing buds for soil nutrients.

Usually, as has been said, the characteristics of stock and scion are seen not to be transmitted to one another. But there are apparent exceptions. It has been found that leaf mottling in some plants can be transmitted by grafting. The reason for this is that the mottling is due to a virus disease, and when a graft is made transmission of the virus takes place. Virus diseases of potato, tomato, tobacco, and many other crop and garden plants are well known and cause very serious losses. The transmission of these has been studied, and tomato and potato are favorable plants for this kind of experiment.

You can graft tomato and potato by cleft grafting. For the scion, use a shoot a few inches long and remove most of the leaves except the smallest. Then cut the base of the shoot neatly to a sharp point (Figure 21). Select a suitable plant, not too young or too woody, for the stock, cut off the main shoot at a point where the diameter of stock and scion is the same, and then make a vertical cut in the end. Place the scion in this cut and bind the two together with raffia (previously softened with warm water) so that both are firmly held together. Keep the grafted plant away from the direct sun for a few days. In the case of tomatoes and potatoes, the union will take up to about two weeks to complete.

If you have a tomato or potato plant with leaf mottling, or a potato with leaf roll or some other suspected virus disease, you can try transmitting it in this way. If similar symptoms are transmitted, you have good evidence that you are dealing with a virus infection.

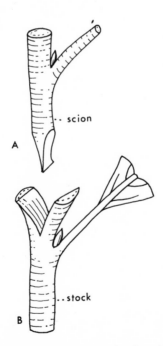

FIGURE 21.    *Cleft grafting for potato and other similar plants.*

Another, perhaps easier, way of grafting such plants as tomatoes, cucumbers, and other plants that have long flexible stems is *inarching*. A notch is made in each stem, one pointing upwards and the other downwards. One is then slipped into the other (Figure 22) and the graft tied up as before. When the union is complete, one or the other of the stems may be cut so that either plant can be made the scion or stock as desired.

FIGURE 22.   *Inarch grafting.*

# 13 | Soil Bacteria

Soil is anything but the inert material it appears to be. It is teeming with living organisms, most of them so minute that they can be seen only with the aid of a microscope. Even the larger organisms such as earthworms, nematodes, and insect larvae are far more numerous than one might think. An acre of field may contain as many or more than 50,000 earthworms alone. The smallest organisms are the bacteria, all-important because they bring about the processes of decay through which the dead remains of organisms are broken down to their original components to be used again by living organisms. One can show the presence of living organisms in soil by observing the changes they bring about. Milk is turned sour by bacteria, and this can be made the basis of a simple experiment.

Take a small amount of garden soil, sift out all stones, twigs, and the like and divide it into two halves. Put a spoonful or two into a small tray and bake it in an oven. Then take two conical (Erlenmeyer) flasks or narrow-necked bottles and boil water in them for ten minutes or so. Boil also some milk in a saucepan for a few minutes, empty the flasks of their boiling water, add immediately a little of the boiled milk to each and plug both the flasks at once with a light plug of fresh clean cotton. Carefully remove one of the cotton plugs, holding it in your hand all the time, shake a little of the baked soil into the flask, and then replug. In the same way add a similar quantity of unbaked soil to the other flask and replug. Keep both in a warm place for a day or so and then remove the plugs and smell the milk. What do you observe? Can you offer an explanation for your observations?

Some of the most important and interesting bacteria are those concerned with nitrogen fixation; i.e., the uptake of nitrogen from the atmosphere and its incorporation in the body of the bacterium. There are really two categories of these bacteria—those that live in association with other plants and those that are free living. Dig up a clover, vetch, or alfalfa plant from a field, or, if you prefer, a pea or bean from your garden. Look at the roots carefully and you will find they bear small swellings or nodules (Figure 23). These nodules contain bacteria that are able to absorb and use the nitrogen of the air that is present in the soil. The bacteria convert the nitrogen of the air into water-soluble nitrogen compounds that the plant can use. So the Leguminosae, the family to which these plants belong, has an advantage over the rest of the plant world in this respect, and many can flourish where the combined nitrogen content of the soil is very low. This association is also one of the reasons for growing clover, alfalfa, and other legumes as fodder crops. If the roots are plowed under, the soil is enriched in nitrogen, in addition to the yield of the crop itself.

Quite simple experiments can show that the root nodules do not form in soil in which all organisms have been killed. Take a quantity of soil sufficient to fill a five- or six-inch planting pot and sterilize the soil by boiling it in water for ten minutes in an open saucepan of sufficient size to prevent boiling over. Then gently boil the excess water away until the soil is dry enough to put in a really clean pot. Fill another similar pot with ordinary unsterilized soil and sow equal numbers of runner beans or peas in each. Allow them to

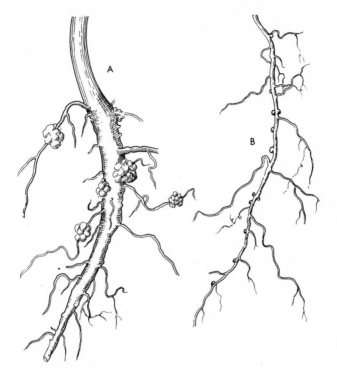

FIGURE 23. *Roots of lupin and clover showing bacteria nodules.*

grow till they are about a foot high (one-third of a meter) and then tip the plants out of the pots and wash away the soil from the roots. What do you observe? If you have a microscope, you can try making a preparation (Chapter 14) of one of the nodules to see the bacteria. However, these are very small, and you will need a microscope with an oil immersion objective.

There are other bacteria that fix nitrogen directly in the soil as well as those that do it in association with the Leguminosae. One of these is *Azotobacter,* and it can be made the basis of some interesting experiments.

*Azotobacter* is a bacterium that needs the presence of oxygen and will grow on the surface of soil, provided the nutrients it requires are present and the surface does not dry up. If conditions are really favorable, the bacteria grow and divide to form a tiny pearly rounded colony large enough to be seen with the naked eye. Other organisms, such as molds, may grow as well, but they are quite different in appearance. You can count the bacterial colonies.

To carry out the experiment, you require the following chemicals: potassium phosphate (dihydrogen phosphate), acid potassium phosphate, some mannitol, and some precipitated chalk. You may have the phosphates in a chemistry set. If not, they are not expensive and are easily obtained. If mannitol cannot be obtained, starch can be used instead. Rice starch is best because it has the smallest grains and all the chemicals should be finely powdered. You will require a number of small containers such as pill vials. They should have a diameter of about one inch or so (3–4 cm.), and to make the best comparisons they should all be the same size.

The two phosphates supply potassium and phosphorus, which are both essentials for bacterial growth. One, however, is rather acid, the other alkaline, but since *Azotobacter* prefers the neutral or slightly alkaline conditions it is best to make a mixture of the two, which should be close to neutral. Mix thoroughly two parts by weight of potassium phosphate with one part by weight of potassium acid phosphate. Dissolve one part of this in 1,000 parts of distilled water, say one gram in a liter of water. Shake well to get the salts to dissolve. This should be neutral, but you can test it with any of several indicators. If on testing it is not neutral, you can carefully add a little of one or other of the phosphates until it is. If you cannot get distilled water, use clear filtered rain water. Tap water may be used, but it is usually alkaline, and so a larger proportion of the acid phosphate will be required to achieve neutrality.

Take a quantity of good garden soil sufficient to fill the number of containers you have decided to use, and spread the soil out to dry in the air. Good garden soil is most likely to contain *Azotobacter,* but nearly all soil, barring the most acid, does. Then sift the soil to remove the stones, roots, etc., and divide it into two halves. To one half add about 1 percent of mannitol by weight, or if you are using starch, about five times as much.

Now divide the soil sample with mannitol (or starch) in four equal portions. Prepare each of the four portions as follows:

1. Make a soil paste (mud) with distilled water.
2. Make a soil paste (mud) with phosphate solution.
3. Make a soil paste (mud) with distilled water and a little chalk.
4. Make a soil paste (mud) with phosphate solution and a little chalk.

Put each of the above into a vial. Smooth off the top with a knife or spatula to make as flat a surface as possible. Don't forget to label the vials (1, 2, 3, 4).

Repeat the steps with the soil sample that has no mannitol or starch.

You will then have eight mud pies as follows:

| *No mannitol* | *With mannitol* |
|---|---|
| 1. Soil only | Soil only |
| 2. Soil+phosphate | Soil+phosphate |
| 3. Soil+chalk | Soil+chalk |
| 4. Soil+chalk+phosphate | Soil+chalk+phosphate |

Place the vials of moist soil in a moderately warm place, but not so warm as to make the surfaces dry up. In fact, cover the surfaces to prevent this, but do not allow the cover to touch the surfaces of the soil. Keeping the pots moist is very important. The soil in each of the pots should be uniformly wetted. If it dries out, no colonies of *Azotobacter* will appear. After forty-eight hours, count the number of colonies on each surface with the aid of a hand lens, and compare them carefully to see if the addition of mannitol or chalk or phosphate produce any significant increases. Take colony counts at intervals until growth of the colonies appears to stop. Table eight shows some typical results.

TABLE 8—The numbers of Azotobacter colonies on a garden soil

| Treatment | No. of colonies | Average | Increase or decrease |
|---|---|---|---|
| None (control) | 15 | 15 | — |
| Chalk only | 33 | 33 | +18 |
| Phosphate only | 71 | 71 | +56 |
| Chalk and phosphate | 122 | 122 | +107 |
| Mannitol alone | 144, 150, 149, 160 | 150 | |
| Mannitol and chalk | 166, 162, 253, 180 | 190 | +40 |
| Mannitol and phosphate | 350, 470, 425, 175 | 355 | +205 |
| Mannitol and phosphate and chalk | 359, 276, 225, 376 | 309 | +159 |

# 14 | The Use of
# the Microscope

The use of a microscope can add a great deal to your study of plants. It is not necessary to spend a small fortune to obtain a microscope. The problem is not so much of finding one to buy, but of choosing from the wide variety of good instruments that are available at low and moderate cost. A detailed description of the features of microscopes is beyond the scope of this book, but a few matters that could apply to the purchase of one may be in order. Beware of exaggerated claims of magnification. The magnification obtained with a compound microscope is the product of the magnification of the objective lenses and the eyepiece lens. It is possible to "blow up" the magnification with higher power eyepieces, but if the optics are low quality, the resultant image is nothing more than a blur.

There are many microscopes sold in "kits." These are usually made of plastic and may be sold in toy departments of stores. Most of these are poor, but there are a few fairly good ones. Always try before you buy. Be wary of instruments with undersized objectives. Examine carefully a microscope with a "zoom" type eyepiece. The zoom eyepiece enables you to change magnification without changing the objective or eyepiece lens. However, a well-constructed zoom lens adds to the price of a microscope, and a zoom lens on a low-priced instrument may not last. Test out the mechanical parts. Do the focusing adjustments move easily, but firmly? When you focus the microscope does the image remain in focus or does it "drift" out? The latter is indicative of poor construction. Some microscopes have light sources built into the base. If you consider one of these, ask the dealer if he stocks replacement bulbs, and if so, buy a few if you buy the microscope. If the dealer does not have spare bulbs, the situation is probably that they are not available, and you may do well to consider another instrument or another dealer. Check to see if the lenses are coated to reduce chromatic aberration (rings of color in the image).

Any microscope you are likely to buy will be one that utilizes transmitted light. That is, the light passes through the specimen and then through the lenses to your eye. This means that specimens you examine will have to be thin enough for light to pass through. Much of the preparation of specimens for microscopic examination is directed to making the specimens thin enough to be transparent.

A long discourse on how to use the microscope is not appropriate here. There are many variations in microscope construction and the details of use vary accordingly. Basically, it is necessary to get sufficient light passing through the specimen and to bring the lens system into focus for your eye. The higher the magnification, the smaller is the field of view and less light will get through the lens system. It is usually best to survey your field of view with low power before using higher powers to examine particular things more closely. Objects on the periphery of the field of view will be "lost" on changing to a higher power. If you are going to use a microscope for long periods of time, try to get used to keeping both eyes open. This is rather difficult to do at first, and a good training technique is to cover one eye with a hand. Observing with one eye closed for long periods results in eye muscle strain and possibly headaches.

Visit a small pond, or a stagnant puddle, and collect some green pond scum, as it is usually called. Using a pocket lens you can see that it consists of fine green threads. Place a very few of these in a drop of water on a microscope slide, cutting them, if necessary, with a sharp penknife. Take a cover slip, touch the drop of water with one side of it while supporting the other side with a mounted needle (Figure 24). Then lower the cover glass gently on to the slide and your preparation is ready. This procedure helps to eliminate air bubbles. The drop of water should be just sufficient to form a film between the cover glass and the slide. Any excess should be carefully removed with blotting paper, and there must never be any water on top of the cover glass.

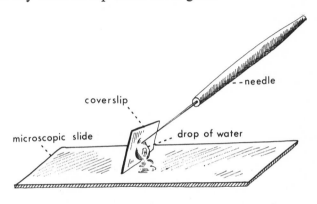

FIGURE 24.

You will notice the fine threads of the plant to be made of cells, and they may look something like the drawings in Figure 25. *Cladophora* is a very common pond scum, usually rather yellow-green in appearance and rough to the touch. *Spirogyra* is a bright dark green and smooth and silky to the touch, and there are many others.

There are much smaller forms of plant life than the visible threads of pond scums. The green powder you can see on tree trunks is a tiny one-celled organism called *Pleurococcus* which can be mounted easily and examined. There are many others to be seen in pond and river water, and some of them are free-swimming.

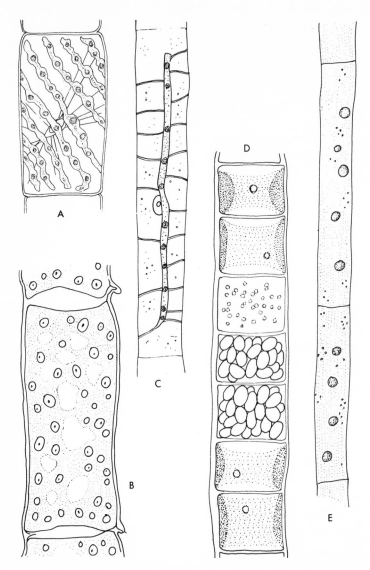

FIGURE 25.   *Various kinds of algae found in fresh water* (*A*) Spirogyra, (*B*) Cladophora glomerata, (*C*) Mougeotia capucina, (*D*) Ulothrix aequalis, (*E*) Mougeotia viridis.

A classic investigation is the observation of the cells of onion "skin." Cut an onion into quarters. Remove a concave section and break it. Gently pull the section apart and strip out the transparent membrane between the "leaves." Cut a small piece of the membrane and place it in a drop of water on a slide. With needles, flatten the membrane as much as possible. Mount with a cover slip. At low power, you should clearly observe the cell walls and the large vacuole in the cells. To observe the nucleus and possibly other cell parts, it is necessary to stain the preparation. Iodine solution or tincture of iodine is a good stain and is readily available. Place a drop of iodine on the slide right next to one side of the cover slip. Do not put the stain on the cover slip. Hold a small piece of blotting paper or paper toweling in contact with the opposite side of the cover slip so as to draw the water out from under the cover slip (Figure 26). The iodine solution should move in to replace the water. Repeat the operation if necessary.

The iodine should stain the nuclei a brown color, and if you look carefully, you may be able to see one or more *nucleoli* (sing. *nucleolus*) within the nuclei.

There are many more cells you can easily observe. One of the easiest things to see are the cells from the pith of a berry, and almost any one will do. Scrape a very tiny quantity of the pith on to a slide in a drop of water and mount with a cover slip. It is also useful to stain with iodine. These cells should show the outer envelope or cell wall, the nucleus, stained brown by iodine, occasional chloroplasts (green bodies), and starch grains, stained bluish black with iodine. The whole of the central part of the cell which looks empty is

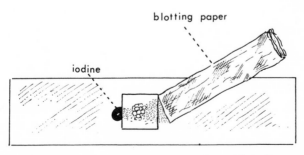

FIGURE 26.   *Irrigating a preparation with iodine.*

full of cell sap, while the wall is lined on the inside by a layer of living material, the cytoplasm, in which the nucleus is embedded (Figure 27).

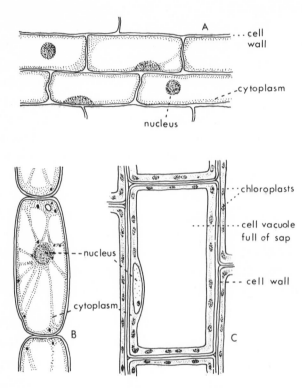

FIGURE 27.   *Three examples of plant cells (A) onion, (B) spiderwort, (C) typical leaf cell.*

Other things to examine with a microscope include the leaves of *Elodea*. Take a young leaf of this water plant and mount it in a drop of water. Then find the midrib of longer cells and focus very carefully on the chloroplasts in them with the high power. They will be seen to be slowly moving around the cell, carried by the cytoplasm. Try to see if the direction of circulation is the same in all cells, and see if you can measure the time a chloroplast takes to travel around

one cell. Protoplasmic movement may also be seen in many
other plants (Figure 28).

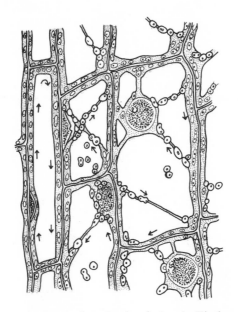

FIGURE 28.   *Protoplasmic circulation in* Elodea.

Easy microscopic objects to examine include the hairs on
the leaves and stems of plants for these can easily be scraped
off with a knife or needle and mounted as before. Here again
a little staining is helpful. Plant hairs may be simple, one-
celled unbranched structures, or multi-cellular outgrowths
looking like miniature trees; they may be glandular with cells
at the head that secrete substances of various kinds, or even
more complex like the stinging hairs of a nettle (Figure 29).

Pollen grains are also easy things to examine with a microscope. Just shake or rub a little of the pollen from the stamen
of a flower onto a microscope slide and examine them first
as dry objects, then mounted in water, and then mounted in
a stain (e.g., safranin) dissolved in alcohol. This stain, and
most others, can be bought as a prepared solution. Pollen
grains have an outer wall called the *extine,* which is variously

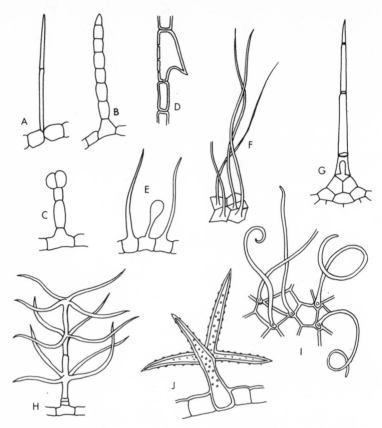

FIGURE 29. *Different kinds of plant hairs.* (*A*) *corolla of* Epigaea, (*B*) *leaf of* Coreopsis, (*C*) *corolla of* Phryma, (*D*) *leaf of* Avena, (*E*) *calyx of* Heliotropium, (*F*) *stem of* Onopordum, (*G*) *leaf of* Cucumis, (*H*) *young leaf of* Platanus, (*I*) *fruit of* Rubus, (*J*) *stem of* Aubretia.

sculptured, and an inner wall or *intine,* which is thinner. At maturity the pollen grain contains two nuclei, but they are difficult to see even with staining. Occasionally, you can see them as in the spiderwort (*Tradescantia virginiana*), where one nucleus is long and narrow and the other small and spherical, especially if a nuclear stain like acetic methyl green in used (Figure 30).

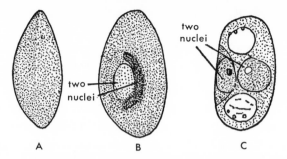

two
nuclei

two
nuclei

A                    B                    C

FIGURE 30.   *Pollen grains of spiderwort.*

You can also try to germinate some pollen grains in sugar
solution. Many pollen grains germinate in a sugar solution
if it is of the right strength. Though this is rather a matter of
trial and error, the following concentrations are suggested.

Peony, 5% sugar

Spiderwort, 5–8% sugar

Sweet pea, other peas, and the tulip, 15% sugar

Onion (*Allium*), 5% sugar

A 5 percent sugar solution is made by dissolving 5 grams of
table sugar in 100 ml. of water. Other percentages of solution
are made accordingly. Place a drop of this mixture on a slide,
and shake in some pollen grains. Mount with a cover slip.
Better still, a hanging drop culture may be set up as this
allows of a better supply of oxygen to the grains (Figure 31).
This is set up by using a small plastic ring which is stuck
onto a slide with petroleum jelly. A thin drop of the sugar
mixture is placed on a cover slip, and the pollen grain sprin-
kled on to it. This slip is now sealed to the ring face downwards using a little petroleum jelly. Care should be taken to
make the drop a thin one, otherwise it will not be possible

cover slip          hanging drop

petroleum jelly          glass or plastic ring

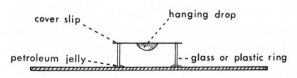

FIGURE 31.   *A hanging drop culture.*

to focus sufficiently far down with the high power to see the pollen grains.

You can also use depression slides and dispense with the plastic ring. The cover slip, with the drop of solution, is inverted and mounted over the depression in the slide.

Another way to grow pollen is to place the sugar solution in a saucer, and on the top of this float a small square (about 1 cm.) of thin cellophane, on the top of which the pollen is scattered. Another saucer is then placed on top to keep the preparation humid, and after a few hours or longer, the cellophane squares are transferred to a microscope slide, a cover slip placed in position, and the preparations examined.

Protoplasmic circulation can often be seen in the tubes produced by pollen grains, often very beautifully. Most pollen grains develop within hours of being sown on the right sugar solution, and some grow very quickly indeed. The green house plant *Gloxinia* (*Sinningia speciosa*) has grains that germinate in 10 percent sugar solution in about two hours, and grow so rapidly that with strong magnification many observers have claimed that the tip can be seen to move across the field of view. Such observations require enough patience to keep your eyes glued to the microscope for several minutes (Figure 32).

Other interesting observations can be made by cutting thin sections of plant material. With a single-edged razor blade, cut as thin a slice of potato tuber as you possibly can. Place it in a drop of water and mount with a cover glass. If you carefully focus up and down with the fine adjustment, you may be able to observe the facets or the multi-sided cells. If you stain with iodine, you may be able to see the individual starch grains within the cells. The study of the cells and tissues of living things is called histology.

Cutting thin slices is the key to examining the microstructure of plants. A laboratory instrument that is designed for cutting very thin slices is called a *microtome*. Some microtomes can cut incredibly thin slices; sections of five microns or less are not at all uncommon (a micron is $\frac{1}{1,000}$th of a millimeter, or about $\frac{1}{25,000}$th of an inch).

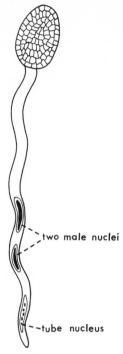

two male nuclei

tube nucleus

FIGURE 32. *Germinating pollen grain.*

In the plant histology laboratory, some rather elaborate procedures are carried out to obtain thin sections of plant tissues and to stain and mount the sections of slides. Among these procedures are embedding in paraffin (or other similar material) to "hold" the tissue for thin sectioning, staining to bring out certain features, and permanent mounting on slides. With a single-edged razor blade or other suitable cutting instrument, you can make reasonably thin sections of small stems, leaves, and flower parts. An interesting investigation is to cut a long section of a flower pistil that has been pollinated. You might be able to see the pollen tubes. Try various staining materials you may have. In some instances, even food coloring will stain differentially; that is, stain certain parts and not others.

Refer to the Bibliography for books that have detailed instructions on histological techniques.

# 15 | Ferns, Mosses, and Liverworts

Many of the small green plants growing on the ground, on tree trunks and on rocks belong to the group of plants known as Bryophyta. This includes two distinct sub-groups; the mosses and liverworts. They should not be confused with lichens which grow in similar places as mosses but which are gray-green, yellow, or black, but never a really bright green. You can easily make your own collection of mosses. Just allow them to dry, and they will keep indefinitely packed away in small envelopes. When you want to look at them soak them for a while in water, and they will swell and appear as fresh as when they were first gathered. Mosses make excellent subjects for study with the microscope. Mount a single moss leaf quite flat in a drop of dilute glycerine under a cover slip. It is not all that easy, but in good preparations you can see the whole size and proportions of the leaf, the size and shape of the individual cells, the character of the margin, the pattern of the midrib if present, and many other features (Figure 33).

It is also not too difficult to grow many mosses—to make a moss garden, in fact. You must, of course, try to imitate the original conditions in which you find the moss. For example, most grow well in a moist atmosphere and do not thrive in bright sunshine. Many mosses will grow in shallow trays with

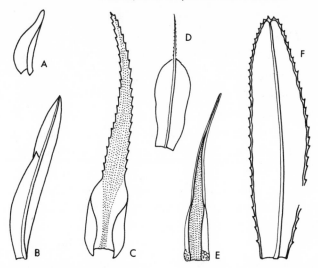

FIGURE 33. *Moss leaves.* (*A*) Andreaea petrophela, (*B*) Fissidens polyphyllus, (*C*) Polytrichum alpinum, (*D*) Tortula intermedia, (*E*) Campylopus schwarzii, (*F*) Mnium affine.

a little soil on which you can put a layer of stones, or small fragments of rocks or peat or sand or rotten wood, according to the species you wish to grow. The mosses should just be pressed into this, but they should have a little of their original soil adhering to them. They should be watered frequently and covered with a glass plate. This prevents the mosses drying out in hot weather. The tray of moss should be kept in a place sheltered from the wind and also from too high temperatures, but much of this you will learn through trial and error. Some mosses will grow much better than others. You will find it necessary to remove ordinary plants as "weeds," and it will probably also be necessary to remove some of the mosses that grow too fast to give the more choice mosses you wish to grow a better chance. Covered aquarium tanks or large brandy snifters are good for growing mosses. When used in this way the container is called a terrarium.

Some of your mosses will almost certainly form capsules that release many tiny spores that ultimately grow into new moss plants. These capsules have elaborate structures that aid and regulate the dispersal of the spores. Each capsule usually has a hoodlike cap which drops off to reveal the lid of the capsule. When the lid is cast off, a ring is left (sometimes double) of what are called peristome teeth. These peristome teeth are fascinating objects to see with a microscope, and the variation in them to be seen in different species is quite amazing. Find a capsule and look at it as a dry object on a slide; then cut the peristome off the top of the moss capsule with a sharp razor blade, and again look at it with the microscope as a dry object. The actual detail will depend on the particular moss you have chosen, but some examples of moss peristomes are shown in Figure 34.

The teeth of the peristome are very sensitive to slight changes in the humidity of the air. These movements can easily be seen by breathing on a capsule and observing the peristome with a lens or the low power of the microscope. In some peristomes the teeth bend inwards in moist air and outwards in dry, in others inwards in dry and outwards in moist air. The outward bending allows the spores to escape; but in some peristomes there is a second insensitive set of teeth that act as a sieve and allow the spores to escape gradually.

You can make use of your ability to grow mosses to investigate the spore dispersal. Take a long seed tray or box and fill it with sterile compost. Press the surface down with a block of wood so as to make it smooth. Plant a row of moss cushions along one of the short sides of the box, using a species that is near to ripening its capsules. Tilt the box slightly as in the diagram (Figure 35). When the capsules are ripe produce a draft of air with a hair dryer (in the cool position) or an electric fan for a few minutes. Keep the soil surface moist and covered as for a moss garden, and later you may see small plants springing up. Before this happens you may see a kind of green color on the surface of the soil. This is called the moss *protonema*. A moss spore first produces a green threadlike growth on which buds are formed

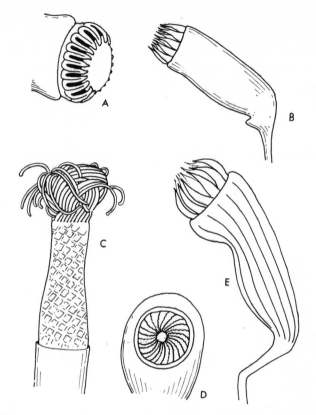

FIGURE 34. *Peristome teeth of mosses* (*A*) Catharinea undulata, (*B*) Cynodontium virens, (*C*) Tortula subulata, (*D*) Amblydon dealbata, (*E*) Timmia austriaca.

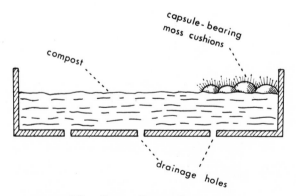

FIGURE 35. *Spore dispersal in mosses.*

which grow into new leafy moss plants. You may be able to take off some of the threads of the protonema and to examine them with the microscope.

Alternatively, you can germinate the moss spores and obtain the protonema directly. To do this, take a small dish or saucer and several thicknesses of blotting paper to fit it so as to make a firm pad. Moisten this thoroughly. Now take some ripe capsules, break them up and scatter the spores on to the blotting paper. Cover the dish and take care to see that it does not dry up. In a short time the protonema should be seen on the surface of the blotting paper, and you can examine it with the microscope. It consists of branched filaments and often some of the cross walls of the cells are oblique; in the axils of the branches some tiny buds develop which grow into new leafy moss plants (Figure 36).

Ferns, commonly seen growing in woody areas, are representatives of a class of plants that flourished as large plants in the Carboniferous Period over 350,000,000 years ago. Even today, in tropical regions, there are tree ferns that reach a height of sixty feet or more.

Ferns are vascular plants, that is, they have tubes in their roots, stems, and leaves that conduct water. They do not produce seeds but, like mosses, reproduce by means of spores.

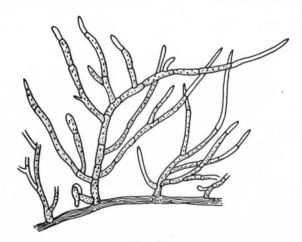

FIGURE 36.   *Protonema.*

The spores are produced on the undersides of the leaves in structures called *sori*. Sori are generally black, but some are brown or even reddish. They can be seen, usually, in late summer. When the spores fall to the ground they germinate into a small vaguely heart-shaped plant called a *prothallus*. The prothallus has structures that produce sperm cells and egg cells. When an egg cell is fertilized by a sperm cell, a new leafy fern plant is the eventual result. This type of reproduction, referred to as *alternation of generations,* is quite common among plants and is observed in some animal groups as well.

What we ordinarily call a fern is the *sporophyte,* that is, the phase that produces *asexually* by means of spores. The *prothallus* that forms from the spore is the *gametophyte* and reproduces sexually, with sperm cells and egg cells to produce another sporophyte generation. In mosses, the leafy plant is the gametophyte and the capsule and stalk is the sporophyte. Seed-forming plants also exhibit alternation of generations, but it is not as obvious as in mosses and ferns.

Ferns can be collected if you are prepared to do a bit of digging. Ferns have an underground stem called a *rhizome,* which can extend horizontally for a foot or more. Rhizomes vary in size with the species, but generally the larger the fern, the larger the rhizome. It is important that the rhizome and the roots not be damaged. Dig in a roughly circular pattern around the leafy frond. The diameter of the circle must be big enough to take in the rhizome with a considerable amount of soil around it and the roots. Wrap moist newspaper around the roots and rhizomes. Transplant the fern in large clay pots lined with gravel on the bottom. The soil in the pots can be soil from the collection area or made up of equal parts of sand, peat, and loam. Keep in subdued light and water enough to keep the soil moist but not soaking.

You can try to grow fern gametophytes. The following is only one of many possible methods. Be warned that this is a difficult procedure that requires much care and patience.

Select a fairly large clay planting pot and fill to within

about two inches of the top with bits of broken flower pot, or stones or gravel. Cover to the top with good-quality loam. Gently pour boiling water over the pot to sterilize it. Take care not to disturb the sand too much. Sprinkle spores on the sand by crushing some sori to release the spores. Cover the pot with clear plastic wrap and place the pot in a bowl of water. The wrap should not touch the soil. Keep the pot in moderate to dim light.

It will take about three or four weeks for the prothalli to grow. The prothalli can be seen with the unaided eye, but you will need a magnifying glass or microscope to examine them closely.

If you can keep the prothalli going for four or five months, you can try to grow sporophytes from the prothalli. Carefully transfer single prothalli, with a little soil attached, to pots of rich soil. Water moderately. Allow another three or four months for sporophytes to develop. If mold grows in your preparations (usually because the soil is too wet), water with 0.01 percent potassium permanganate solution.

# 16 | The Fungi

When fungi are mentioned very likely the first examples that come to mind are the common edible mushroom and the toadstools found in nature. Actually, the toadstool or mushroom is only the fruiting or reproductive body of the fungus; what might be called the real plant body consists of many fine white threads growing in the soil and can often be seen adhering to the base of the toadstool as you pull it from the ground. The toadstool produces literally millions of spores from the flat radiating plates or gills on the underside of the cap. The spores are minute and are carried everywhere by air currents, and so the fungus is dispersed.

All biologists do not agree that fungi are plants. Many classify fungi as *protists,* maintaining that in order to be called a plant the organism must make its own food. There are exceptions to this, such as the Indian peace pipe which has no chlorophyll.

The spores vary in color with the kind of fungus, and you can make "spore prints" of them. To do this, dip some sheets of white paper separately in melted paraffin wax in a flat dish; then hold them up so that the excess wax drains away and allow them to dry. Then take a fresh toadstool, cut or break away the cap from the stalk and place it with the underside downwards on the sheets of waxed paper for two or three days. Spores by the millions will drop from the gills and form a pattern of radiating lines on the paper which is a reflection of the pattern of the gills themselves. If you *gently* warm the paper, the wax will melt just sufficiently to stick the spores in position, and you will have a permanent record of this particular fungus. The spore print and the color of the spores are characteristic of different species. You can make a collection of spore prints. One thing you will find is that the color of the spores is not necessarily the color of the gills.

You can try making similar prints with other plants that produce spores; for example, ferns. The sori contain many *sporangia,* which are tiny spherical boxes that contain many spores. The sporangia can be seen with a pocket lens. Each of these sporangia springs open to liberate the spores, which, although larger than the spores of fungi, are still produced in vast numbers. Spore prints can be made for these in the same way as for the fungi, but the spores of ferns are all of a similar brown color, and the interest of the spore prints lies in the fact that they show different patterns reflecting the shape and arrangement of the sori on the underside of the leaf.

Mushrooms and toadstools mostly live on the dead remains of plants and animals and are consequently known as *sapro-phytes.* There are many other smaller fungi which live in the same way; for example, the molds that frequently grow on foodstuffs such as bread and cheese, as well as on dead leaves and fruits and other material undergoing decay. Any one of these molds can be examined with the microscope. The blue-green mold so common on rotten oranges and other rotting foods is a *Penicillium,* though it is not the kind from which penicillin is obtained, which is a much rarer species. Some fungi are *parasites,* growing on living organisms.

It is fairly easy to grow some of the aquatic fungi that are saprophytic. To do this some food material is required, and for this you can use almost anything. Good choices for first attempts are a small piece of apple, or a soaked seed or a piece of cooked egg white. Whatever you decide to use, tie it to a piece of thread and suspend it in the middle of a large jar full of fresh pond or river water. After a few days a fine white mold will be seen growing from the bait. This mold looks like thin cotton, and some of it can be transferred as gently as possible to a microscope slide and examined with the microscope. Most of the aquatic fungi obtained in this way are species of *Saprolegnia, Achyla, Pythium,* and you can see the fine tubes (called *hyphae*) with the high power of the microscope.

Many of the aquatic fungi reproduce by setting free very tiny little spores that are able to swim about in the water and that ultimately give rise to new fungi. You may be lucky to see these in the water, but if not try applying a little pressure to the cover slip. This may be just enough to release some of them from one or two of the hyphae so that you can see them.

*Saprolegnia* does not always live on dead materials; occasionally it attacks the gills of fish causing what is called "salmon disease." It also attacks the body surface of the fish if it has been injured and some of the protective scales have been knocked off. Here the fungus is living as a parasite and causes a disease; numerous other diseases, particularly of plants, are caused by fungi.

One such disease is caused by a fungus related to *Saprolegnia* called *Pythium* and it causes the "damping-off disease" of seedlings. If seedlings, like cress, tomato, or snapdragon, are sown close together, kept covered with a glass cover so that the internal atmosphere is moist and warm, then they may develop a brownish region just above soil level, fall over, and die. Some of these infected parts can be mounted on a microscope slide and crushed by a little pressure on the cover slip. The fungus can be seen growing between the cells of the seedling, particularly if a little stain such as cotton blue is added to the preparation.

One of the most important fungus diseases is potato blight. It is a fungus that changed the course of history for it caused the Irish famine in 1844–45. Many thousands of people had to leave Ireland. Many came to the United States.

Careful examination of numerous wild and garden plants will show you many examples of plant diseases, which you can examine with your microscope. Mildews are often seen as white molds on leaves, while the brown streaks on the leaves of grasses and cereals are known as rusts. In diseases known as bunts, the ovaries are transformed into masses of black or dark-colored spores. Try looking for these on some of the common wild grasses, such as the false oat or the cultivated cereals like barley.

# Appendices

## SOME ANSWERS AND COMMENTS
## ON THE QUESTIONS
## ASKED IN THIS BOOK

*Page 5*

Plants will usually not grow well in soil that has been previously sown with the same plant. A different plant should do better in the "used" soil.

Moist soil should support plant growth better than dry soil.

Materials such as grass mowings, leaves, etc., act as fertilizers and should improve plant growth.

*Page 25*

In nature many species of seeds have to go through cold winters. This is a survival adaptation and provides a better chance for germination in the spring when conditions are favorable.

*Page 28*

The fifteen-minute standing time should allow the enzyme mixture to catalyze the breakdown of the starch so that a positive test for starch should not occur.

*Page 54–59* MENDEL PEA EXPERIMENTS

The bud should be removed since fertilization may already have taken place. Following is a brief summary of some aspects of Mendel's work as it applies to the investigation described in Chapter 9. For a more complete discussion of Gregor Mendel and his work, refer to genetics books and biographies of Mendel. Several references are listed in the Bibliography.

When Mendel crossed the round seed plants with the wrinkled seed plants, the first generation of offspring plants all bore round seeds. When these seeds were planted and the plants allowed to self-pollinate, their offspring (the second generation) bore round and wrinkled seeds in a ratio of three round to one wrinkled. Mendel surmised that the round characteristic was somehow dominant to the wrinkled characteristic. He surmised further that the characteristics separated when the gametes (pollen and egg cells) were formed and recombined in the offspring so that the offspring inherited two factors for each characteristic.

The crosses can be represented as follows:

R=round seeds   r=wrinkled seeds (recessive characteristic is represented by a small letter)

First cross pollination RR X rr

$F_1$ (first generation) Rr Rr Rr Rr all seeds round since the factor or gene for round seeds is dominant.

The self-pollination of the first generation is represented:

Rr X Rr

$F_2$ (second generation) RR Rr Rr rr

RR is round, Rr is round and rr is wrinkled. Therefore, the ratio of round seeds to wrinkled seeds is 3:1.

Writing down the probabilities of two traits at a time is referred to as a dihybrid cross

R=round   r=wrinkled   Y=yellow cotyledon   y=green cotyledon

First cross pollination:   RRYY X rryy

first generation: ($F_1$)   RrYy all round, yellow

Self-pollination of $F_1$   RrYy X RrYy

|      | RY       | Ry       | rY       | ry       |
|------|----------|----------|----------|----------|
| RY   | RR YY    | RR Yy    | Rr YY    | Rr Yy    |
| Ry   | RR Yy    | RR yy    | Rr Yy    | Rr yy    |
| rY   | Rr YY    | Rr Yy    | rr YY    | rr Yy    |
| ry   | Rr Yy    | Rr yy    | rr Yy    | rr yy    |

The probabilities are:

9 round yellow to

3 round green to

3 wrinkled yellow to

1 wrinkled green

Refer to genetics books for Chi square calculations to determine the validity of your results.

These results show that in Mendelian inheritance, the inheritance of one characteristic is not dependent upon the inheritance of another. This is Mendel's law of random assortment. Refer to discussions of *linkage* for explanations of apparent contradictions of this law.

*Page 70*

Plants should grow best in red and blue light and, of course, in white light. They should grow poorest in green light. Leaves are green because the wave lengths we perceive as green are reflected from the surface. Since the green light is not absorbed, it cannot provide energy for photosynthesis.

BUFFERS

Phosphate Buffer (Gomori) (0.2 Molar)
Make up the following stock solutions:
27.6 grams of monobasic sodium phosphate ($NaH_2PO_4$) dissolved in 1,000 ml. of distilled water.
53.6 grams of dibasic sodium phosphate ($Na_2HPO_4$) dissolved in 1,000 ml. of distilled water.
For the desired pH, mix the amounts as indicated in the table:

| pH | $NaH_2PO_4$ ml. | $Na_2HPO_4$ ml. |
|---|---|---|
| 5.9 | 90.0 | 10.0 |
| 6.1 | 85.0 | 15.0 |
| 6.3 | 77.0 | 23.0 |
| 6.5 | 68.0 | 32.0 |
| 6.7 | 57.0 | 32.0 |
| 6.9 | 45.0 | 55.0 |
| 7.1 | 33.0 | 67.0 |
| 7.3 | 23.0 | 77.0 |
| 7.4 | 29.0 | 81.0 |
| 7.5 | 16.0 | 84.0 |
| 7.7 | 10.0 | 90.0 |

# BIBLIOGRAPHY

The books are grouped into general categories. In some instances the contents of a book make it appropriate for more than one category.

*General Reference*
Coulter, Merle C. and Howard Dittmer. *The Story of the Plant Kingdom*. Chicago: University of Chicago Press, 1964.
Klein, R. M. and D. T. Klein. *Discovering Plants*. Garden City, N.Y.: Natural History Press, 1968.
Novak, F. A. *The Pictorial Encyclopedia of Plants and Flowers*. New York: Crown, 1966.
Cronquist, A. *Introductory Botany*. New York: Harper and Row, 1961.
Maesfield, G. B. et. al. *The Oxford Book of Food Plants*. New York: Oxford University Press, 1969.
Fernald, Merritt, Lyndon. *Gray's Manual of Botany*. New York: American Book Co., 1966.
Esau, Katherine. *Plant Anatomy*. New York: John Wiley and Sons, 1965.
Hylander, Clarence J. *The World of Plant Life*. New York: Macmillan Co., 1956.

*Ecology*
Hay, John and Peter Farb. *The Atlantic Shore: Human and Natural History from Long Island to Labrador*. New York: Harper and Row, 1966.
Pohlgren, John and Cathleen Pohlgren. *Backyard Safari*. Garden City, N.Y.: Doubleday & Co., 1971.

Watts, Mary T. *Reading the Landscape: An Adventure in Ecology.* New York: Macmillan Co., 1957.

McCormick, Jack. *The Living Forest.* New York: Harper and Row, 1959.

Pringle, Laurence P. *Discovering the Outdoors: A Nature and Science Guide to Investigating Life in Fields, Forests and Ponds.* Garden City, N.Y.: Natural History Press, 1969.

Wier, Ester. *The White Oak.* New York: McKay, 1971.

Tubbs, Colin R. *The New Forest: An Ecological History.* New York: Transatlantic Arts, 1969.

Boughey, Arthur S. *Fundamental Ecology.* Scranton, Pa.: Intext, 1971.

Olson, Sigurd and Les Blacklock. *The Hidden Forest.* New York: Viking Press, 1969.

Teal, John and Mildred Teal. *Life and Death of the Salt Marsh.* Boston: Little, Brown, 1969.


*Soils*

Sullivan, G. J. and J. W. Batten. *Soils: Their Nature, Classes, Distribution, Uses and Care.* University, Ala.: University of Alabama Press, 1970.

Alexander, M. *Introduction to Soil Microbiology.* New York: John Wiley and Sons, 1961 (also a good source for fungi and bacteria).

Buckman, Harry and Nyle C. Brady. *The Nature and Properties of Soils.* New York: Macmillan Co., 1969.

Millar, C. E. and L. M. Turk and H. D. Foth. *Fundamentals of Soil Science.* New York: John Wiley and Sons, 1965.


*Biochemistry, Physiology, and Nutrition*

Devlin, Robert M. *Plant Physiology.* New York: Reinhold, 1966.

Galston, Arthur. *The Life of the Green Plant.* Englewood Cliffs, N.J.: Prentice-Hall, 1964.

Stiles, Walter. *An Introduction to the Principles of Plant Physiology.* New York: Barnes & Noble, 1969.

Rosenberg, Jerome L. *Photosynthesis: The Basic Process of Food-Making in Green Plants.* New York: Holt, Rinehart and Winston, 1965.


*Genetics and Reproduction*

Meuse, Bestiaan. *The Story of Pollination.* New York: Ronald Press, 1961.

Budlong, Ware and Mark Fleitzer. *Experimenting with Seeds and Plants.* New York: Putnam's, 1970.

Klein, Aaron. *Threads of Life: Genetics from Darwin to DNA.* Garden City, N.Y.: Natural History Press, 1970.

Brewbaker, James L. *Agricultural Genetics.* Englewood Cliffs, N.J.: Prentice-Hall, 1964.

Paterson, P. *Applied Genetics.* Garden City, N.Y.: Doubleday & Co., 1966.

Stern, Curt and Eva Sherwood. *The Origin of Genetics: A Mendel Source Book.* San Francisco: Freeman, 1966.

Strickberger, Monroe. *Experiments in Genetics With Drosophila.* New York: John Wiley and Sons, 1964.


*Identification and Classification (Taxonomy)*

Benson, Lyman. *Plant Taxonomy: Methods and Principles.* New York: Ronald Press, 1962.

Jaques, Harry E. *Plant Families: How to Know Them.* Dubuque, Iowa: W. C. Brown, 1949.

Lamb, Edgar and Brian Lamb. *The Pocket Encyclopedia of Cacti and Succulents in Color.* New York: Macmillan Co., 1970.

Morley, Brian D. *Wild Flowers of the World.* New York: Putnam's, 1970.

Prescott, Gerald W. *How to Know the Fresh-Water Algae.* Dubuque, Iowa: W. C. Brown (this title can, of course, be used as a general reference for algae).

Montgomery, F. H. *Trees of the Northern United States and Canada.* New York: Warne & Co., 1971.

Cuthbert, M. J. *How to Know the Fall Flowers.* Dubuque, Iowa: W. C. Brown, 1948.

————. *How to Know the Spring Flowers.* Dubuque, Iowa: W. C. Brown, 1948.

Lemmon, Robert S. and Charles C. Johnson. *Wild Flowers of North America in Full Color.* New York: Doubleday & Co., 1961.

Dawson, E. Yale. *How to Know the Seaweeds.* Dubuque, Iowa: W. C. Brown, 1956.


*Growing Plants*

Cruso, Thalassa. *Making Things Grow Indoors.* New York: Knopf, 1970.

————. *Making Things Grow Outdoors.* New York: Knopf, 1971.

Kramer, Jack. *Gardens Under Glass: The Miniature Greenhouse in Bottle, Bowl, or Glass.* New York: Simon and Schuster, 1969.

Graf, Alfred B. *Exotic Plant Manual: Fascinating Plants to Live With—Their Requirements, Propagation and Use.* New York: Charles Scribner's Sons, 1970.

Wellman, Frederick. *Plant Diseases, an Introduction for the Layman.* Garden City, N.Y.: Natural History Press, 1971 (also has information on fungi).

Kranz, Frederick and Jacqueline Kranz. *Gardening Indoors Under Lights.* New York: Viking Press, 1971.

Wyman, Donald. *Wyman's Gardening Encyclopedia.* New York: Macmillan Co., 1971.

Abraham, George. *The Green Thumb Book of Indoor Gardening.* Englewood Cliffs, N.J.: Prentice-Hall, 1967.

Graff, M. M. *Flowers in the Wintergarden.* Garden City, N.Y.: Doubleday & Co., 1966.

Schneider, G. W. and C. C. Scarborough. *Fruit Growing.* Englewood Cliffs, N.J.: Prentice-Hall, 1959 (has some information on budding and grafting).

*Algae, Bacteria, and Fungi*

Gray, William D. *The Relationship of Fungi to Human Affairs.* New York: Holt, Rinehart, and Winston, 1959.

Christensen, Clyde M. *The Molds and Man: An Introduction to the Fungi.* Minneapolis: University of Minnesota Press, 1956.

Hutchins, Ross E. *Plants Without Leaves.* New York: Dodd-Mead, 1966.

Smith, Alexander H. *The Mushroom Hunter's Field Guide.* Ann Arbor, Mich.: University of Michigan Press, 1963 (also useful for mushroom classification).

Stone, A. Harris and I. Leskowitz. *Microbes are Something Else.* Englewood Cliffs, N.J.: Prentice-Hall, 1970.

*Ferns, Mosses, and Liverworts*

Bland, John H. *Forests of Lilliput: The Realm of Mosses and Lichens.* Englewood Cliffs, N.J.: Prentice-Hall, 1971 (since lichens are a symbiotic relationship between fungi and algae, this book is also a reference for these organisms).

Sterling, Dorothy. *The Story of Mosses, Ferns and Mushrooms.* Garden City, N.Y.: Doubleday & Co., 1955.

Durand, Herbert. *Field Book of Common Ferns, For Identifying Fifty Conspicuous Species of Eastern America With Directions for Their Culture.* New York: Putnam's, 1949.

Wherry, Edgar T. *The Fern Guide: Northeastern and Midland United States and Adjacent Canada.* Garden City, N.Y.: Doubleday & Co., 1961.

————. *The Southern Fern Guide: Southeastern and Midland United States.* Garden City, N.Y.: Doubleday & Co., 1961.

Cobb, Boughton. *A Field Guide to the Ferns and Their Related Families of Northeastern and Central North America, with a Section on Species also found in the British Isles and Europe* (Peterson Field Guide Series). Boston: Houghton-Mifflin Co., 1956.


*Use of the Microscope and Microtechnique*

Sass, John E. *Botanical Microtechnique.* Ames, Iowa: Iowa State University Press, 1958.

Gray, Peter. *Handbook of Basic Microtechniques.* New York: McGraw-Hill, 1964.

Needham, George H. *The Microscope: A Practical Guide.* Springfield, Ill.: Charles C. Thomas Co., 1968.

# Index

DR. C. T. PRIME was formerly Chief Biology Master and Chief Science Master at the Whitgift School in England. Since his retirement he is self-employed as a writer, lecturer, and examiner. He is the author of several books on botany, including one on woodland ecology, and of articles in scientific journals. AARON E. KLEIN is a science writer and editor who has taught science at both public schools and universities. Among other books he has written several laboratory manuals in science.